AUTHENTIC
YOUTH MINISTRY

Straight Talk about Working with Kids, Teens & In-Betweens

CASSIE MOORE

CONCORDIA PUBLISHING HOUSE · SAINT LOUIS

Published by Concordia Publishing House
3558 S. Jefferson Avenue, St. Louis, MO 63118-3968
1-800-325-3040 • www.cph.org

Manufactured in the United States of America

1 2 3 4 5 6 7 8 9 10   25 24 23 22 21 20 19 18 17 16

Table of Contents

Introduction

Twenty faces swiveled toward me, eagerly anticipating my lesson. I stood confidently, ready to inspire the entire classroom of inquisitive teenagers.

Yeah, right.

Let me tell you what *really* happened when I faced a classroom of students for the very first time.

I stood uncertainly in the front of the classroom, watching twenty middle schoolers clamber over desks and chuck books and erasers at one another.

When I attempted to get their attention, one student actually sat down.

I mentally congratulated myself for capturing her attention. Then I realized she merely paused to tie her shoe before launching herself back into the mayhem.

Contrary to what I would have called it under my breath, this was Sunday School. It felt more like a swarming school of piranhas, hungry to devour every last shred of my resolve.

My first attempt at leading students was a dismal failure. I walked out of the room with no clue about what to do. And believe me, the last thing I needed was some expert in a book or video lecturing me about all the ways I was inadequate as a volunteer.

That's precisely why you won't find that in this book.

Here's the truth: I get it. I walked in your shoes. I volunteered to lead children and youth, and I still do.

Currently, I serve as a middle school religion teacher and youth worker. Before that, I led youth programs, taught school, and did everything in between. I worked in classrooms of five students and auditoriums of hundreds in summer camps, Sunday School, youth gatherings, mission trips, and service projects.

I understand the stress, apprehension, confusion, and frustration of leading young people. I dealt with drama, tears, discipline issues, awkwardness, headaches, and tension.

But these challenges often led to great surprises, hearty laughter, and deeper relationships. God gave me the privilege of seeing kids, parents, and whole families grow in grace and knowledge of the Lord Jesus Christ.

I witness attitudes, mind-sets, and behaviors change as people of all ages explore God's Word. Seeing people work together passionately to serve others and make a difference for someone else brings many joys. And experiencing the moment a young person grasps God's grace is, well, priceless.

In years of researching and learning, the most valuable lessons I learned resulted from a lot of trial and error. I'd love to help you avoid some of my mistakes and start with more tools than I did.

The goal of this book is to offer you an all-encompassing how-to guide for working with children and youth, whether you work as a volunteer or as a professional youth worker.

I hope you understand yourself better as a leader, work more confidently with students, and enhance your service in practical ways.

I hope you laugh and learn alongside me. Because trust me, once you've had a kid puke in the back of a rental van stuck in rush-hour traffic, all you can do is chuckle.

Section 1:
You, the leader

Why are you doing this, anyway?

Several thirteen-year-old girls screamed shrilly as I yanked my car to the side of the road. The thump-thump-thump sound was unmistakable. I blew a tire.

Surrounded by cornfields.

On the way to a massive weekend retreat for several hundred participants. That I would lead.

Panicked girls dragged their suitcases out of my trunk and sat on the curb. One accidentally hit the siren button on my emergency bullhorn and shattered my eardrums with a maximum-volume blast. I faced a haunting question. Why am I doing this, anyway?

As a volunteer, you probably asked yourself this very question. Often, we ask this question when everything seems to go wrong, when we're stuck in the doldrums, or when we face a challenging situation.

I never told anyone this, but for a time, I hated my work with kids.

I had plenty of reasons. I was drowning, working too many hours for too little pay. I felt completely burnt out as I juggled endless tasks. I questioned whether my efforts were wasted on a bunch of teenagers who didn't really care. No matter how hard I prepared or how heartfelt my intentions, I didn't see kids impacted the way I expected.

I almost walked away from working with students for good. I started applying for corporate jobs and prepared how to break the news to my youth. I thought, "At least I'm getting paid for this. My poor volunteers actually have it worse than I do."

In the midst of the darkness of self-doubt and frustration, God worked a big change in my heart.

Just a week before I planned to announce my decision, I experienced my first-ever mission trip. I led a group of rambunctious, troublemaking middle schoolers on one of the muddiest and coldest trips ever.

On that trip, exhausted and muddy, I saw the real heart of my students and fellow leaders. In no uncertain terms, God showed me that the vocation of working with children and teens may not be glamorous or logical, but it's truly the most important job we can do.

Let's be honest. Yes, it's hard.

Youth simultaneously break your heart and renew your joy over and over again. You may travel through periods of doubt, anger, and questioning. You may find it difficult to see the fruit of your efforts. You may feel like you never have enough time to get everything done.

People question why you waste your time. "Why do you bother? And when are you going to get a real job?"

And you may struggle financially. I once broke out in tears in the cereal aisle of my grocery store because I realized my low-paying youth ministry job meant I needed a big coupon to buy a box of my favorite cereal.

But, friends, it's the most rewarding work a person can do.

As God's children, what we offer our students is vastly important. More critical than fame, success, or achievement, we communicate God's love, acceptance, forgiveness, and future. Christ's death and resurrection frees us from our bondage of sin and invites us into an eternity in heaven. Nothing in the universe comes close to the importance of this truth. And God empowers us to share it with the people surrounding us. What a privilege!

My students admit that they deeply admire volunteers and leaders who dedicate their time to work with them. They value you more than you could ever guess.

A student once wrote to me, "My leaders have been like parents to me, teaching me things I don't know. They've also been like my brothers and sisters, being there for me in the hard times. They're also my friends, because I can tell them jokes and still have fun with them."

"I think my leaders are amazing for all they do," says high school student Grace. "I'm so happy to talk to you and be open. I know you can't fix my problems, but it's just nice knowing that someone cares and has had the same experiences. You give me the feeling that everything will be okay and that God is really there."

Countless others echo the same appreciation for adults who understand, care, and share their wisdom and concern. They silently love that they can trust and confide in you. They quietly respect our desire for them to learn and grow, even though it sometimes doesn't seem like it.

As a middle schooler once told me, "My leaders really helped me see God. I became a Christian because of the influence of godly volunteers in my life who believed in relationships and not just religion."

What kids want from their leaders

In an act of sheer bravery, I asked a former youth to give me her hold-nothing-back opinion of several years of youth events.

Jules, now a hardworking college student, agreed to discuss the years she spent as one of my students. As we joked about her willingness to speak the truth bluntly, I asked her to tell about her favorite youth events.

She thought for a moment and then replied, "Quite honestly, my entire life was impacted just hanging out with you."

She went on to explain that though she enjoyed our zany youth events, her life was profoundly affected by spending time next to me, watching me tackle the ups and downs of my life. Through countless hours together, she reveled in the relationship of a Christian adult and the mutual sharing of advice, trust, and care between us.

Until then, I disregarded the hours I spent driving kids to events, sitting next to them at football games, and chatting over coffee. It turned out that these daily routines I took for granted offered the biggest testament of faith to Jules.

You see, I'm far from perfect. You only have to see me drive in rush-hour traffic to confirm my many faults. But I learned that one of the most important things I can do as a leader is to invite students into my life. When they see the real me struggle, doubt, and fumble, they relate to me in a deeper way. Because, in the midst of our wreckage as sinful people, the Holy Spirit still works and shines forth through us.

As St. Paul said in 2 Corinthians 12:9, "[The Lord] said to me, 'My grace is sufficient for you, for My power is made perfect in weakness.' Therefore I will boast all the more gladly of my weaknesses, so that the power of Christ may rest upon me."

As leaders, it's our duty to peer beneath the surface of our kids' lives and recognize what they really need from us. Just like the tiniest tip of an iceberg peeking above the water masks the gigantic mass invisible in the depths below, our students only show us a small portion of who they are, what they're really thinking, and what their life truly entails.

See the deeper hurts. Whether it's a cheerful straight-A all-star who cries herself to sleep every night or a cocky football player who desperately wants someone to be proud of him, we have the opportunity to carefully pry away the thick walls of protection our kids have built up and apply the healing balm of the Gospel to their hurting hearts.

It doesn't matter if you're the most skilled speaker in the world or write the best lessons since Socrates. If you don't stay connected to your kids and seek to understand what's going on beneath the surface, you won't impact them as you hope.

Very insightful students tell me they deeply value the youth leaders in their lives. Over and over, when I ask what they want most from leaders in their lives, students indicate a desire to have someone to trust and confide in, someone who will love them no matter how badly they mess up.

As teenager Brennen summed up for me, "I want my youth leader to be someone who is easy to talk to and who tells you what you need to know. I need them to be there for me when I need them most and to understand how I feel."

Several times over the last few years, I asked students what they value most from their leaders. Their answers fall into a few general categories.

Trust

Overwhelmingly, students most desire to be able to trust their leaders.

One girl in my small group said it best. "The most important thing I need in a leader is trust. I have to be able to tell them anything and everything." Our kids need unshakable confidence in us. They need to know we are trustworthy and care enough about them to handle whatever they throw at us.

It can be challenging to hear confidential information about kids, their families, and their situations, but it's vital to be caring leaders no matter what they tell us. In trusting us, their walls of defense gradually lower and we have the opportunity to help fix broken hearts and hurt feelings.

Guidance

Childhood, and especially adolescence, presents some of the most confusing challenges of our lives.

Our students attempt to balance rapidly changing emotional, social, physical, intellectual, developmental, and spiritual changes with brains that aren't fully developed. No matter how well adjusted a child may seem, he or she still needs a lot of guidance to navigate this difficult journey.

As middle schooler Emily admitted, "I want my youth leaders to be like a friend and to give me wisdom when I need it. I also want to talk to someone who gets my generation and is able to understand our needs."

In a time when everything seems to be changing, we can offer soothing influence and point to an unchanging Creator. We can remind our students that others have been through the same challenges and survived just fine.

Challenge

Our students are sponges, soaking up knowledge quickly. They're hungry to learn, grow, and be challenged.

One of the most tragic mistakes we make is failing to recognize the potential of our kids. We often do this in the form of the "Oh, someday" phrase: "Oh, someday you'll be a great leader" or "Oh, someday you'll actually understand what it means to work hard." When we say phrases like these to kids, we convey a subtle attitude of superiority.

Why not instead speak the truth now, and encourage kids who already show leadership potential at a young age? Or point out that we appreciate the hard work they put in with homework? Although not "adult issues," young people already face significant situations. Don't discount their struggles.

By recognizing personalities, affirming effort, and challenging kids to take the next step in growth, we help inspire a younger generation instead of dismissing them. Our children are far more capable than we give them credit for, so set your standards high for them.

A good listener

Many times, I felt the pang of insignificance when someone I talked with mentally checked out.

You know, that moment when a person lets their eyes roam, looking for other people to converse with.

Scores of kids say one of the most highly desired traits of a youth leader is being a good listener. Actively listening to kids and teens shows that we care about them. Don't just wait for students to finish talking so you can jump in with your own stories. Pay attention, nod, and ask questions. Sometimes kids just want someone, anyone, to show genuine interest in them.

As one of my youth related, "Just knowing that there is someone there that you can talk to about life in general is comforting."

Loving support

One of the most poignant responses received from students about what they wanted from their leaders simply stated, "I want them to love me no matter what I do."

Our kids desperately need our support as they get their balance in this challenging world. On a daily basis, they struggle in a world that makes them second-guess everything about themselves, including their looks, technology, relationships, and young personalities.

As leaders, we need to help lift them up gently when they fall to their knees, wobbly and unsure that they can stand. We must constantly cheer them on and remind them that no matter what happens, they have a loving God who walks with them through the ups and downs of life. And we're right there in the storms for them too.

Understanding

Kids often think no one in the world quite understands them.

Middle school and high school students especially struggle with feeling misunderstood. They are all too aware that many adults fear working with them. Paradoxically, students long for someone to confide in and someone who will attempt to understand them.

As teenager Erin explained, "I like when a leader understands your thought process and understands what it's like to be this age." By asking questions, paying attention to their unique likes and dislikes, and diving into their world, we show that we care about them. Every single person in this world desires to know that they matter. Show your students that they matter to you.

A role model

Many of my students are older now and lead ministries of their own. One of the most delightful experiences of my life was taking my current students, young teenagers from Florida, to a mission organization in St. Louis led by my former students.

As I watched my former students minister to this younger generation, I was blown away by how many of my catchphrases and teaching habits they apparently picked up and absorbed into their persona as leaders.

Parents of children are likely aware of this odd feeling. Imagine hearing your own words from the mouths of others and seeing your actions mirrored by someone else. It's bizarre!

This experience reminded me afresh of how closely our students study us, and our vast amount of influence on them. Our actions speak volumes to the kids in our lives. Even the smallest unthinking action, such as shaking your fist while driving with kids in your van, or sneaking a cookie when you think no one's looking, impacts those who watch to see that our words and actions align.

Our students desperately want to look up to caring, thoughtful adults who value them, listen to them, and love and support them. As one of my students confided, "I want someone who I can trust and talk to about my life, someone who really understands and cares about what we think."

That person who makes such a profound impact in the lives of kids and youth is you.

Signs that you're a leader

*I almost got suspended in middle school
for leading a dress-code mutiny.*

Our private school adopted a strict dress code over the summer. This required assembling new wardrobes to meet the stringent criteria. By decree, we had to wear solid-color polo shirts with absolutely no logo of any kind.

Of course, what did I have an abundance of in my closet? Polo shirts with logos.

Thinking creatively, I purchased a roll of smiley-face stickers and carefully applied a sticker over the logo on my shirt. When none of my teachers said anything about skirting the dress code, I started passing stickers out to my classmates. At my urging, nearly my entire grade regularly applied stickers to their shirts.

Despite an enthusiastic grassroots campaign, my actions finally caught the ire of my teachers. As they threatened suspension, one teacher pulled me aside and said, "Leading is a gift. Don't misuse it."

Let me say something that may challenge the way you view yourself: you are a valuable leader.

Some of you might resist that word. You may think you're not really a leader. Often, people shrug and tell me, "Nah, I'm just a volunteer. I'm not that important." For some reason, they feel unworthy or unwilling to see themselves as a leader.

No, my friends.

If you're using your God-given gifts and talents to guide others in some manner, you're a leader.

Making the seemingly innocuous shift to view yourself as a leader can subtly change how you see yourself and the important role you play in the lives of students you work with.

I'd like to challenge you to think about why you volunteered in the first place. Did you see an unmet need that no one else did anything about? Do you have a deep desire to make things better? Perhaps you felt frustrated with the current condition of a program and thought you could tackle it better than those already serving. Maybe you have a natural gift for working with kids. Or did something happen in your life to launch you onto this path?

Whatever your particular journey, one of the best starting points in leading children and youth is to first examine yourself. As Aristotle said, "Knowing yourself is the beginning of all wisdom." And St. Paul exhorted, "Examine yourselves, to see whether you are in the faith. Test yourselves. Or do you not realize this about yourselves, that Jesus Christ is in you?—unless indeed you fail to meet the test!" (2 Corinthians 13:5).

I believe every person on this planet asks themselves two questions at some point: Who am I? And what is my purpose?

Understanding who you are and defining your purpose are key foundations in your role as a leader.

You don't have to lie on a couch and squint at inkblot tests, but a deeper understanding of how your personality, passions, and talents converge to make you unique will help you thrive in your role.

I once penned a journal entry detailing how I was pretty sure I knew how it felt to jump into the sea wearing a ball gown and holding a twenty-five-pound sack of flour over my head while trying to tread water.

I suspect most of you can relate, though I'm not claiming we're Navy SEALS.

My point is that most everyone I know runs a million miles a minute on a daily basis. We tread water while attempting to juggle many heavy challenges all at once—jobs, health, families, relationships, finances, and spiritual lives.

Too often, we don't make ourselves much of a priority. Generally, the majority of people who volunteer have a deep love for others. This can mean we regularly get booted to the end of the line as we first take care of everyone else. Many of us neglect ourselves and don't take time to think about our own well-being.

Assessing yourself as honestly as possible sometimes means gathering insights from those around you, including friends, co-workers, and even your students. They can help you learn more about yourself.

While I would be the first to say that you can't base your entire opinion of yourself on what other people say about you or how they react to you, it's worth carefully considering these things and attempting to draw some conclusions. Take a deep breath, and find a quiet place to think seriously as you continue reading.

Let's take a quick look at what makes you . . . well, *you*.

Figure out who you are as a leader

Apparently, I'm fondly known as "The Clipboard Lady."

Walking around a farmers market, sporting a jaunty cap and a carefree attitude, I ran into members from my church.

When they spotted me, the first thing out of their mouths was "Wow, it's so nice to see you outside of work, looking so relaxed, without responsibility, or even a clipboard!"

This reminder showed that people often view me as the responsible, always-in-charge adult. The organized person with a clipboard. The leader running events with the precision of a drill sergeant. (Hey, my students' words, not mine.)

A friend once bluntly said, "Cassie, you can't be in the boat without steering it."

Ouch! The truth hurts, doesn't it? His candid words identified the kind of leader I am, a take-charge person who leads others naturally. And to be honest, an occasionally pushy and strong-willed one who doesn't always do so well taking instruction from others.

It's not always so easy to figure out who we are as youth leaders. Whether you've been schooled, trained, or thrown into your first few weeks of volunteering, it's daunting to nail down who you are as a guide of others.

Working with kids and youth can serve as a powerful mirror. It's hard to escape the truth of who we are when we work with observant youth who freely make unfiltered comments on the good, the bad, and the ugly of our personalities.

An old saying asserts that children are the only members of humanity who really tell the truth. Those who work with kids know this is most certainly true. They just don't filter anything they say. And if you spend much time with them, to the point where they feel even remotely comfortable around you, they tell you exactly what they think about you. Their words can give insight to who you are, how you treat others, and how you influence others.

With that kind of scrutiny, it's no wonder they can tell when we feel excited or angry, when something didn't work out the way we planned, and when we want to throttle an obnoxious thirteen-year-old who won't stop throwing baseballs at the projector.

I teach middle schoolers on a daily basis, and they know exactly when I'm ticked off. In fact, they can probably see my irritation building before I even notice. I used to have one particular student who would occasionally turn to our rowdy group with a deadly serious face and announce, "Guys, knock it off. Cassie is reaching her limits of putting up with our baloney."

The fact is, people around us know us better than we give them credit for. They know the kind of people we are and how we lead. Their remarks can provide valuable insight. Those truths, when we actually listen to them with thoughtful consideration, can propel us to more self-awareness. This can make us more thoughtful and effective servants in God's kingdom.

Are you introverted or extroverted? Do you get excited about organizing events, or would you rather spend time playing hockey with your youth? Do you lead by example as a servant, or do you prefer to inspire others with your passionate words? What drives you batty, what makes you tick, and what makes you proud? What are your strengths and where do you need to improve as a leader? Start listening for the answers to these important questions.

I'll pick on myself for a moment. In listening to my students joke about my inability to deal with inefficiency over the years, I realized I have an extremely short fuse when it comes to disorganization. A few years ago, I rented vans for a mission trip and the rental company bungled my careful plans. It got ugly when I realized that they botched the paperwork and gave me a van without air conditioning to transport youth from Texas to St. Louis in the middle of a hot, sticky summer.

I learned to counteract my personality by placing jolly and good-natured leaders around me. I find people who roll with the punches, precisely because I don't always roll so easily.

In the case of the steaming-hot rental van, my happy-go-lucky leaders came to the rescue and made the trip fun, even though I felt irritated. Instead of my personality ruining the trip, it became a bonding experience (albeit a smelly one).

Of course, listening to how others perceive our leadership doesn't end with just hearing from the people around you. It also means throwing yourself into God's Word and listening to the truth of who you are in Christ through Scripture.

It's fascinating to me how human nature so often clouds the beauty of our Savior. I think of it as a lighthouse. We're lighthouses with dirty windows that we stubbornly refuse to clean. Sometimes we don't even realize how disgusting our windows are, because we're powerless to reach up and clean them on our own. Sometimes we can only see dirt and the crooked and crude drawings we etched in the filth.

Christ the beacon shines from within those lighthouses. Unfailingly bright, He warmly illuminates everything, shining in the midst of darkness. His light never dims, but shines faithfully. Even though the grime of our dirty windows sometimes conceals His glow, His light continues zealous illumination.

When we finally see our grimy and gritty windows, admit our filth, and allow the cleansing of the Gospel, Christ shines ever more brightly.

Knowing our windows are dirty is a valuable truth for youth leaders. It helps us face the fact that we're sinful people, full of failure, who desperately need a Savior to forgive us and cleanse us.

So who are you, according to God? In 1 Peter 2:9, He tells us, "You are a chosen race, a royal priesthood, a holy nation, a people for His own possession, that you may proclaim the excellencies of Him who called you out of darkness into His marvelous light."

Listen to the feedback from the people around you. Learn from them and from Scripture about your leadership skills, tendencies, and weaknesses. Then take that knowledge and prayerfully apply it to your life. Pray for God to wipe the grit and dirt off your windows so that others may see the glorious glow of our Savior through you.

As Matthew 5:16 so beautifully reminds us, "In the same way, let your light shine before others, so that they may see your good works and give glory to your Father who is in heaven."

Know your personality

Adaptable. Creative. Persistent.

Quick! If you had to describe yourself to others in just three words, what would you say?

Our heavenly Father crafted each one of us lovingly with a vast array of quirks and features. Though not perfect—you're still a sinful human being in desperate need of a Savior—you're perfectly able to reach those around you in your own special way.

Your personality bears significant importance on who you are as a leader and how you serve. It contributes to your leadership style, and your gifts and talents make you a unique force to reckon with.

One important distinction identifies whether you're an extrovert or introvert. Knowing which one you are teaches you how to recharge properly when you feel drained.

Many people inaccurately think extroverts are wildly outgoing, love being around lots of people, and never stop yammering, while introverts prefer to curl up inside with their cat and a book and ignore the text messages.

More accurately, extroverts draw energy from being around others, while introverts feel drained by them. Plenty of introverts love people and communicate effectively but need time to recharge after spending time with others. Likewise, many extroverts love solitude but are invigorated when in busy social settings.

Let me give you an example from my life. I'm a strong extrovert. That means I physically have to hold myself back from talking to strangers while waiting in the checkout line at a store. I feel more geared up while teaching or hanging out with friends than when I engage in a solitary activity.

My husband, on the other hand, is a strong introvert. He's a pastor and a very engaging public speaker. He can act like a total goofball and life of the party, but he needs alone time to reenergize. Dealing with others wipes him out.

Understanding your inclination toward introversion or extroversion helps immensely in ministry. You can more easily recognize situations that energize you and circumstances that drain you. You can identify habits to implement in your daily life to help you thrive as a leader.

In addition, it's helpful to realize people recharge differently, depending on whether they're introverts or extroverts. The simple understanding of this personality characteristic can greatly enhance your relationship with other volunteers, co-workers, parents, children, friends, and siblings.

I recently jetted across the country to attend a work conference with a good friend, Nick. We made the grueling seven-hour flight home after working for several days. I jabbered away happily because my extrovert personality thrives on being around other people.

Nick, the introvert, kindly removed himself from my chattering presence to wander the airport for an hour in solitude. Because we understand the differences between our personalities, neither felt offended by the other's behavior.

I frequently encourage my co-workers and leaders to take a bevy of personality tests, because it's so helpful to understand yourself when you spend time serving others. As Carla H. Krueger said, "The greatest barrier to self-understanding is our fear of knowing the truth within ourselves, but when we do understand ourselves, we greatly enhance what we are capable of."

Find your passions

What you feel most strongly about usually defines your passions.

So what compelling desire inspires you or ignites intense emotion? What gives you life? What ignites your excitement just by thinking about it? What gets you fired up and motivated to act?

Identify your passions another way by considering what you would do for free, or what you would do with your time if you had no other responsibilities. Perhaps you're passionate about teaching survival skills to teenagers, to develop independence and self-sufficiency if they get stranded in the woods. Or maybe you feel passionate about helping children learn about music and dance, so you spend your free time listening to songs and choreographing moves.

Whatever you find yourself drawn to, take note of it. The timing might not be perfect right now to indulge in this passion. But it may very well be the way God uses you at some point to reach a special group of people or connect with a particular individual.

If that time comes, be prepared to act on it. You may be just the perfect person to truly impact someone else through your unique passion.

Recognize your talents

I'm probably the only ten-year-old you know who received a "cease and desist" order.

I was in elementary school when I realized I had a particular knack for administration. I single-handedly organized a club with my classmates. I wrote advertisements, job descriptions, and mission statements for our little group. Eventually, everyone in my class wanted to be a part of my group.

Naturally, they tattled on me.

My teacher called me to his desk and wearily commanded me to disband the club because the kids who weren't in it complained about feeling left out. "Nonsense," my ten-year-old self protested. "All they need to do to join is fill out an application!"

Alas, my teacher's attempts to stall my organizational zeal were in vain. I went on to develop this talent of administrative skill and use it in every area of my life. Having an early grasp of it gave me a tremendous head start in knowing how to learn about, grow in, and hone my strengths in this area of my life.

Consider your talents. What are you naturally good at? In what areas do you have God-given aptitudes? How can you use these talents to benefit the community around you? For example, you might bake for a special event or put your mechanical ability to use by constructing something.

Study yourself and attempt to learn more about who you are. Remember what excited you as a child or teenager, and consider if this indicates a skill or talent you might unwittingly possess. Ask yourself some serious questions. Perhaps ask your family or close friends or even trusted youth leaders or students to give you some insights. They may help shed some light on what you're gifted at, where you shine brightly and contribute in your own distinctive way.

Take some intentional time away from your hectic life and spend some time in a quiet place where you can actually concentrate. Spend time alone with God, understanding who He created you to be. It's not selfish, and it doesn't take away from your service. A retreat away from your everyday schedule is one of the best ways to strengthen yourself to better serve the world around you.

Focus your mind-set

I envy brain surgeons. Their ability to crack open a head and put something in or take something out seems like a shortcut compared to efforts to do the same in students' brains.

As you prepare yourself for service, mind-set is of critical importance. If I could saw open your skull and plant one bit of wisdom in your brain regarding your role, it would be this: God can use you, but it's not about you. It's about Him.

Too often, we fail to see our own selfish nature. Many times, we think we're being kind and generous and good, when we're actually unknowingly serving our own selfish interests. For instance, have you ever been out to dinner with friends and offered to pay for their meal, all the while hoping that they pick up the tab for the next meal instead of just generously giving without expectation?

As sinful creatures, we stumble and splatter ourselves with messy, sinful situations our entire lives. When it comes to service, we often unwittingly volunteer with a mixture of selfless and selfish motives. Thankfully, the One who created us and knows us intimately understands this. It's for this reason, and countless others, that we desperately need the forgiveness of our Savior, Jesus Christ.

As a teenager, I volunteered regularly at church events. Part of my motive was pure, because I wanted to work with kids and use my skills to help build the Church. The darker side of my motivation, however, wanted to pad my résumé for college. The more I volunteered, the more people praised me for being selfless. And all the while, I felt guilty because ambition, not selflessness, kept me showing up every week for nursery duty.

Do you recognize the struggle with mixed motivations? Do you think service is an easy ticket to success and attention? Would you rather accumulate more social media followers than serve humbly? Do you care more about filling an insecurity by finally being the "cool one" instead of using your gifts to God's glory? Do you serve to look more attractive somehow, not because you care deeply about bettering lives? Would you rather throw yourself into the solitary and rigorous academics of theology so you don't have to live out God's calling to "go and make disciples of all nations"?

I expect that most of us serve with a mixture of selfless and selfish desires. That's why it's all the more important to understand clearly that service is not about us. The Holy Spirit works through us to bless others. You, my friend, are incapable of changing hearts and eternally influencing people, because that's God's role.

Section 1

What a great comfort to know that God understands our greatest strengths and weaknesses, our desires and temptations. Rather than having to explain our complexities and worry about being misunderstood, we can simply surrender to a God who proclaims that He knows even the number of "hairs of your head" (Matthew 10:30).

Just as the moon has no light of its own and merely reflects the light of the blazing sun, we emit no glow on our own and merely reflect God's Son. As we prepare our hearts for service, we must keep this proper perspective in mind to control our own egos.

God can use you, but it's not *about* you. It's about Him.

Curb your attitudes

I was up to my elbows in gritty clay, with dried gunk painfully stuck under my fingernails. Sweaty and tired, I couldn't brush the locks of hair out of my face without smearing my forehead with chunks of brown dirt.

I never figured the hours spent working in an art classroom would teach me the right attitudes for serving others.

The summer after my first year of college, I ambitiously enrolled in a busy art schedule at a local community college. I had high hopes of double-majoring in Christian education and studio art. The only way I could cram all the classes into my academic plan was to tackle summer classes every year.

As I spent hours each day painting, sketching, and working with clay, I experienced a conversation that completely transformed my mind-set about working as a volunteer and eventually serving others in ministry full time.

In my pottery class, I quickly discovered I was the only Christian. As we kneaded clay in the studio, my classmates discussed religion for hours at a time. Yet they didn't care to discuss Christianity.

Arrogantly, I assumed it must be my duty to share my faith with this artistic group. I began to believe God placed me in that class expressly to share the Gospel with unbelievers. I waited eagerly for the chance to share what Jesus meant to me and how His grace had transformed my life as a believer.

Unfortunately, it never came about as I thought it would.

Slowly, after a few weeks of listening to my classmates share their Buddhist, New Age, and atheist beliefs, they started to ask what I believed. Instead of excitedly pouncing into the ring like a sugared-up Easter bunny, I chose my words slowly and carefully. I revealed small bits of God's truth at a time, asking my classmates plenty of questions about their own beliefs as I shared what I believed.

Inside, I constantly felt like I blew it. I didn't make the impact I really wanted to make with these strangers.

At the end of the semester, our entire class took a field trip to a local museum. As we walked around the cavernous rooms, one classmate walked over and asked to talk to me.

We sat down on a bench in front of a giant oil painting. He looked me square in the eyes as he said, "I just want to say thank you. You're the only Christian I've ever met in my entire life that let me speak my mind and didn't try to shove your religion down my throat. It changed the way I see Christianity."

Those words knocked me to my knees mentally.

At that moment, I realized it's not about me. It's all about our Creator.

ISLAM GROWING FASTEST

Muslims are the only major religious group projected to increase faster than the world's population as a whole.

Estimated change in population size, 2010–2050

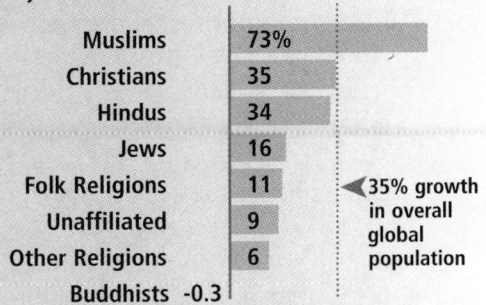

Muslims	73%
Christians	35
Hindus	34
Jews	16
Folk Religions	11
Unaffiliated	9
Other Religions	6
Buddhists	-0.3

◄ 35% growth in overall global population

Source: *The Future of World Religions: Population Growth Projections*, 2010–2050
PEW RESEARCH CENTER

Mistakenly, I assumed I would play a major role in evangelizing to my classmates. I had high hopes of leading the entire group in prayer as they tearfully admitted the Holy Spirit was at work in their lives. My pride sprouted the incorrect view that sharing the Gospel fell all on my shoulders. It was my duty to single-handedly convert my classmates.

In reality, I played a small, infinitesimal role in God's work in these people's lives. Perhaps God only intended for me to soften the heart of this one single man.

Soon after, the words of St. Paul in 1 Corinthians 3:5–9 punched me in the gut. "What then is Apollos? What is Paul? Servants through whom you believed, as the Lord assigned to each. I planted, Apollos watered, but God gave the growth. So neither he who plants nor he who waters is anything, but only God who gives the growth. He who plants and he who waters are one, and each will receive his wages according to his labor. For we are God's fellow workers. You are God's field, God's building."

We serve the almighty, all-powerful God in the ways He prepared for us (Ephesians 2:10). The work of changing hearts? It's up to Him, not us. We need to keep this lesson in mind as we venture into service, my friends.

One of the most insidious sins to infect the Church is the transgression of pride. In fact, the number one piece of wisdom I dole out to people who work with others is to remain humble.

You see, I think the sins of pride and arrogance cripple us most. By nature, pride cuts us off from being teachable or moldable. It prevents us from admitting error or failure. It stops us from connecting with others, sharing credit, and apologizing when needed. It bars us from rolling up our shirtsleeves and doing the required gritty work. Pride whispers, "This is beneath you" and "This really isn't your thing."

Pride keeps us from trying someone else's idea. It isolates us and blocks openness to God's promptings. It makes it difficult to work with others and often prevents others from coming to us. Who wants to confide in someone who sneers down their nose at them?

Most alarmingly, arrogance can veer us off God's path and focus our eyes inward. We count our own kingdoms, accomplishments, and successes, actual or perceived. In my case, the prideful goal to personally convert my entire pottery class to Christianity was terribly misguided.

The very nature of pride makes it nearly impossible to convince someone that they have an issue with superiority. Someone who thinks she knows better than anyone else brushes off helpful remarks, honest assessments, or even harsh criticisms.

I know many servant-hearted people and thank God for them. They are the salt of the earth. I couldn't function without their constant encouragement, love, and care for others. Conversely, pride is a stronghold for many in ministry roles. You see, it's entirely possible to start out with good intentions and slowly become someone who does a disservice to our tender Savior.

We must constantly guard our actions and pay attention to what we allow to settle into our hearts. We must honestly evaluate ourselves and ask those we trust to lovingly critique us. Sin can and does swallow us whole, without us even knowing it happened. Only our ever-forgiving Savior can help us guard our hearts and minds from arrogance. We must never stop going to Him in contrition for our sinful nature.

Throughout college, I served as a resident assistant in charge of a dormitory. During summer training, we cleaned rooms to prepare for the arrival of students. On one particularly hot day, we spent hours scrubbing mold from refrigerators, plunging toilets, mopping floors, painting railings, moving backbreaking piles of mulch, and repainting parking lines.

At one point, I stood panting and exhausted, with a heavy gallon of bleach in one hand. I looked over at our program directors sitting in the shade in beach chairs and sipping ice water. Though they loudly cheered for us, they didn't move from their chairs all day. When our team finished working in the evening, our directors received accolades from the university administration for working so hard.

Their arrogance turned an entire staff of student leaders against them. No pep talk could restore the respect they lost that day.

I shudder to think how many people we turn away because of our arrogance.

Make no mistake, this impacts people's eternal lives. We must remember God didn't call us to lord over a church, place ourselves on a platform, or secretly consider ourselves better than other churches, synods, staffs, or families. Instead, He charged us to "Go therefore and make disciples of all nations, baptizing them in the name of the Father and of the Son and of the Holy Spirit, teaching them to observe all that I have commanded you" (Matthew 28:19–20).

To echo a wise phrase, "We're called to be fishers of men, not keepers of the aquarium."

God commanded us to work in His name alone, not for our glory, but for His. We are merely His beacons, reflecting His light into the darkness of the world around us.

You are not the Savior, but you represent Him to others.

Focus your ministry mind-set on humility. When you focus squarely on lovingly serving those around you with humility, everything else falls more easily into place.

Take care of yourself

I was a swine flu victim.

Remember several years ago when the nation was in the midst of a panic over swine flu?

Media rumors swirled about this giant plague that would overpower our country. Businesses would grind to a halt as people keeled over in their workplaces.

Though it seems hard to believe, I caught swine flu at an apple butter festival in rural Missouri. Well, technically, my husband caught it first, most likely from consuming tainted apple butter samples. He then kindly passed it on to me, rendering me miserably sick for nearly two weeks.

The moral of this story? Never sample apple butter during a modern-day plague, kids.

My swine flu episode tragically aligned with one of the biggest events in my work schedule, a giant retreat I had planned for months. I worked furiously from home, locked in my bedroom, and felt close to fainting on more than one occasion. As I recovered and ultimately attended the retreat, I felt like a zombie stumbling around as a hundred kids ran circles around me.

Why do I tell this story? Because it's critically important to take care of ourselves. As we go into service, mental, physical, and spiritual health matters.

Nearly everyone I know sprints a million miles a minute, every minute of every day. We juggle dozens of tasks and responsibilities every day, managing our jobs, health, finances, families, relationships, and spiritual lives.

Generally, those attracted to ministry roles have a deep desire to serve others. This usually means we end up last in line after taking care of everyone else. How many good people do you know who look neglected and drained because they don't have a moment to stop and think about their own well-being?

I grew up flying all over the country. It always amused me when flight attendants specifically explained the importance of securing your own oxygen mask in an emergency before attempting to help anyone else. It seemed like such a no-brainer! Of course you have to be conscious and safe before trying to help anyone else! Duh!

However, the full implications didn't hit me until I was in my mid-twenties, feeling ground down to a pulp with stress. Suddenly, I realized why I needed to be healthy before attempting to help others. No one can give much of himself or herself to others when they barely cope and feel exhausted.

Take some time to secure your own oxygen mask before helping others. Make an effort to better understand yourself and discover what ignites your passion. Pinpoint what refuels you and what drains you. Face the difficult personal insights.

Are you consumed by unrealistic expectations? Are you too much of a perfectionist? Are you unable to handle the job you committed to do? Are you trapped in an unhealthy relationship that sucks the joy out of life? How do you manage stress? Whether you're a teenager or a grandparent, stress negatively affects you and clouds your brain.

Though I certainly don't have the market cornered on figuring it out and living flawlessly, I picked up a number of insights that helped me balance my life better. Maybe they can help you too.

Mental wellness

My most important tip for taking care of your brain is to never stop being curious.

I think we live happier lives overall if we wonder and want to learn about the big world around us. Ponder new things daily. Make a note in your phone or other device to look into a subject more at a later time.

Read often. The smartest people I know read voraciously; and they advise others to do the same. Through reading, you can discover stimulating new ideas, people, and concepts, especially about subjects that challenge you.

Stay tuned in to the news too. As a leader, it's important to know about current events so you stay relevant to the people you serve. Read community newspapers to catch news about schools, student sports, and local issues. This may even mean reading about a local sports team you don't personally like. Hey, we all need to make sacrifices sometimes!

Being informed is empowering, even if you don't share the knowledge.

Limit time spent on social media. Don't get caught in the numbers game and seek validation by counting followers, friends, likes, shares, and retweets. Avoid comparing yourself with those you connect to online. Your daily grind only looks gloomier when contrasted against someone else's carefully edited and possibly exaggerated highlight.

I find it helpful to declutter my workspace and my house to simplify and refocus my mental energy. I live by the "one touch" rule, which means if I pick something up, I immediately put it where it needs to go, either in its space or in the trash. I also make an effort to unclutter obligations. I learned the hard way that sometimes you have to say no to good things so you can eventually say yes to better things.

Healthy relationships

God created us for community, and the people in yours can be a great blessing to you.

Section 1

My family and friends provide a lifeline to me in times when I feel frustrated, tired, and uncertain. They alternately cheer me on, coach, console, and correct me when needed.

As you tackle daily life, don't forget to spend time with people you love. Meet for dinner. Chat on the phone. Balance your time as an individual with time you spend with others. It does no good to drain yourself needlessly, but especially if you're an extroverted person, spending time with people can be life-giving.

In recent years, I actually added a monthly reminder in my phone to call or text different friends and reconnect. I don't want friendships to slip by the wayside in a hectic schedule.

When dealing with people, don't forget that you may be the only Bible someone ever reads. I make an intentional effort to compliment someone every day, a co-worker, friend, or cashier. By choosing to see the good in people and sometimes spending an extra few minutes to smile and chat with a stranger, you can be a beacon of Christ's love.

Once, I spent an hour talking with a middle-aged woman in the store as we picked out Christmas wrapping paper. She poured out her life story, recounting the pain of a difficult situation, and eventually laughed in embarrassment and said, "This is what happens when someone takes the time to ask how your day is going and actually listens!"

Physical wellness

For busy people, physical activity often becomes the last thing on our to-do list.

Demanding tasks may consume us so much that we fall into bed, exhausted, without even taking time to care for ourselves. Getting enough sleep, eating properly, and getting regular exercise are vital and must become priorities.

I'm not saying to start training for a marathon, but try to create healthy habits. Take the stairs instead of the elevator. Park farther out in the parking lot. Get off the couch and flex during every commercial break. Walk to your co-workers' offices to talk instead of emailing them.

Because physical activity burns stress hormones, it relaxes us and adds to overall health and wellness.

One of my favorite activities is simply getting outside in nature. As a child in rural Illinois, I spent almost every day wandering in the woods, climbing trees, and wading in creeks. That love of nature never left me. It's one thing I do to renew and recharge when I feel drained. Now that I'm an adult, I regularly kayak, walk my dogs, and walk on the beach. Being out in God's creation reminds me that my troubles are temporary. Eternity with the Creator of this beautiful world waits.

Spiritual health

"If the devil can't make you bad, he'll make you busy."

I saw these words on a poster once. They ring true to me. How about you?

Avoid the devil's plots by taking intentional time away from your chaotic schedule to read God's Word, think, and pray. Daily time in God's Word confronts our sin and drives us to the cross to receive Christ's forgiveness. It realigns our thoughts, attitudes, and behaviors to reflect those of our Savior, not the world. God's Word heals, restores, assures, comforts, and empowers us for service. Without regularly diving into God's Word, daily life and its stresses drain us.

Find a quiet place and time to read the Bible and pray. Pick a time when others won't disturb you. If you struggle to find a time, consider using lag time in your schedule, such as commuting, exercising, or waiting. All major digital stores have free Bible apps, and many of these, including Bible Gateway and Faith Comes By Hearing, include audio readings of the text. You may feel surprised at the difference this makes in your life.

I personally struggled for years to read my Bible daily, so I purchased a small hourglass for my desk. I try to find time every day to put aside my work and flip that hourglass over. Until that sand runs out, I'm concentrating solely on Scripture and won't allow anything else to interrupt me.

Make it a point to worship and be in community with other Christians regularly. This is one of the primary ways God strengthens us to serve in our vocations. Flip on Christian music in your car and sing praises while you drive. Partake regularly of the Lord's Supper, where we receive forgiveness of sins in Christ and strength for living as Christians. This Christian food of Word and Sacrament equips us for everyday life as Christians.

Surviving mistakes and overload

I've made a lot of mistakes in ministry, but one of the biggest was throwing food at my kids' heads in a restaurant.

Yeah. Not my proudest moment.

This particular incident took place at the very tail end of a mission trip. I felt exhausted and gritty after three days without a shower. Those who've been with kids for an extended amount of time know that at a certain point, your brain shuts off. You become numb to reason. You begin to congratulate yourself on the mere fact that you managed to keep kids alive instead of staying vigilant and professional.

Section 1

As our large group sat in a restaurant, I had quite enough of my teenage boys and their pesky nagging. Without thinking, I picked up an entire handful of fries and chucked them across the table, right into their faces.

Instead of laughing about it, their jaws dropped and they were rendered speechless. After several uncomfortable seconds of complete silence, I squirmed and said, "What's the problem? Can't I have a bit of fun?"

The silence continued as my teens just stared at me, eyes wide. Finally, one of them quietly said, "We're kids. You're an adult. You can't act like us."

Know what? They were right, and I was wrong.

As I sat in front of them, I realized that sometimes good leaders mess up badly, even when they have the best of intentions. And sometimes, the most important thing you can do is eat a slice of humble pie, 'fess up to a mistake, and say you're sorry.

As a volunteer, you'll make mistakes. It's far easier to minimize shortcomings, rationalize what you did wrong, or even shift the blame onto someone else. And far too often, we compare ourselves with others and comfort ourselves with false hope that we aren't as bad as someone else. But instead of sweeping your mistakes under the rug, humble yourself and admit that you aren't perfect.

Your students don't actually think you're flawless, so they'll feel a deeper emotional connection with you once you open up about your shortcomings. To admit one's mistakes shows strength of character and gives others an opportunity to get things off of their chests too.

And remember, you can learn from every single experience in your life, wonderful, horrible, or in-between.

Romans 8:1–2 reminds us, "There is therefore now no condemnation for those who are in Christ Jesus. For the law of the Spirit of life has set you free in Christ Jesus from the law of sin and death."

Jesus sets us free from the burden of our mess-ups and bad choices. Our mistakes don't have to haunt us or crumble our ministry into a powdery dust. We can stand firm in the truth that no matter what mistakes we make as leaders, our mistakes are washed away and our ministry continues through the power of Jesus.

Sometimes, though, our struggle isn't in blunders, but rather in feeling overwhelmed.

At one point in my ministry career, I worked like a dog, and not one of those cute circus dogs, doing fun tricks to the applause of an adoring crowd. Committed to way too many activities, it seemed as if I simultaneously performed in all three circus rings, flipped and somersaulted as an aerial artist, and directed all the action as ringmaster.

Have you ever been there?

In the midst of my overwhelming workload, I couldn't sleep. I'd lie awake for hours, worrying about my to-do lists. I furiously worked through lunch almost every day, trying to get ahead of my inbox.

More than anything, I wanted to escape. Are some of you at that point too?

I clung to Psalm 61:2 like a life raft, praying along with the psalmist, "From the end of the earth I call to You when my heart is faint. Lead me to the rock that is higher than I."

Unfortunately, there's no magical ten-step solution to give relief from your burden. Instead, I encourage you to immerse yourself in God's Word and in regular worship. So often, we get so busy with great things, many of them related to service and ministry, and we don't take the time to really connect with God in our own lives. Missing time to hear the truth robs us of so much, including a sense of peace and relief.

Look objectively at your schedule and try to determine how you tumbled into this position of overwhelming frustration. Did you add one too many study groups to your week, and you're busting at the seams? Did you volunteer for yet another great opportunity, and now you're stuck? Have your priorities become misaligned? For instance, maybe your passion for helping at-risk kids became lost in the shuffle of a hundred other activities crammed into your week.

Ask yourself if you need to pare down your hectic schedule and focus your energy on fewer things. Saying no to some activities will help focus on work you feel excited to do. Sticking to a more manageable schedule will renew a greater sense of enthusiasm for your work.

As someone once told me, "The fruit grows in the valleys, not on the mountaintops."

Trust me, I know from experience the soul sucking and joy robbing of challenging times. They can plant seeds of intense doubt in your mind. They can make you despair and question if you can carry this burden one more day. They can cause you to push away from people you love, or students you care about, because you fear letting them down.

At these moments of sheer exhaustion, it's often helpful to confide in a friend. Take a serious look at the people God put in your life, and prayerfully consider someone you can safely share your feelings with and who will give you some perspective. God blessed me with a few invaluable friends. I pray He does the same for you.

Let's face it, sometimes we need someone to simply commiserate with us. I learned a valuable lesson from Brian, a dear friend of mine who helped me weather storms by listening to me vent and saying, "This stinks, but you'll get through it."

Section 1

Take heart, knowing that challenging times refine character. God calls us to press forward, despite seemingly insurmountable obstacles. He's the master at delivering His people from them!

One of my favorite Bible verses gives me strength when my days seem long and draining. "Have I not commanded you? Be strong and courageous. Do not be frightened, and do not be dismayed, for the LORD your God is with you wherever you go" (Joshua 1:9).

The frustrating times won't last forever, but the work of the Holy Spirit through you most certainly will. Feelings fade, conflicts resolve, friendships adjust, and responsibilities change, but the work you do through Christ has eternity imprinted on it.

Section 2:
Learning the basics

Dive in!

I'll never forget sitting at my desk the first day of my first professional youth ministry job. Or perhaps more accurately, I'll never forget the overwhelming terror and confusion I felt.

I had graduated from college a few weeks earlier and moved across the country from California to St. Louis, Missouri, where my husband started seminary classes that very week. Still reeling from the effects of hauling furniture up a flight of stairs and cramming it into a too-small apartment, I stared at my computer and wondered where to start.

A million bits of advice, information, options, and possibilities floated into my brain like ash floating down from an exploding volcano. I felt like I might suffocate in the pandemonium of my thoughts. What should I do first? I decided and then persistently second-guessed my decision.

Having started several new roles since that day, I confess that those feelings of being overwhelmed and confused don't necessarily go away. You just learn to work through them.

At times like this, where you start isn't important. What really matters is that you start.

Robert Collier once said, "Success is the sum of small efforts, repeated day in and day out." Just as the situation never will be absolutely perfect to start an exercise regimen or take a vacation, the circumstances in your life will never allow you to easily and flawlessly launch yourself into service. You'll hit bumps, feel tired, get frustrated, and second-guess decisions.

But don't let those hiccups derail you from the incredibly valuable experiences you'll enjoy as you work with children and teens and share in building God's kingdom. Make small efforts, day in and day out.

Now that you know a bit more about who you are and what your purpose is, it's time to prepare yourself for your service. This can be a challenging step to take, and there's no magic formula to use.

Whether you partner with a well-established organization, go through extensive training and preparation, or courageously strike out solo to create a program or role, you need to establish goals and priorities in order to thrive.

Set goals and get started

If the thought of someone lecturing you on how to set goals makes you want to chuck this book across the room, don't worry. You're in good company.

Also, a flying book might seriously hurt someone.

I'll spare you a step-by-step guide, but I'll try to offer practical tips that will make a difference.

You may already have an idea of what you want to accomplish. Perhaps you even know the reason you want to volunteer with kids. To focus your service, I recommend writing a personal philosophy of ministry. Clarifying your intentions lets you reflect on what matters and gives you a sense of purpose and motivation for sharing in God's work.

According to a Japanese proverb, "Vision without action is a daydream. Action without vision is a nightmare."

Most people define a philosophy as a theory or attitude that acts as a guiding principle for behavior. Center your philosophy of ministry around what you consider most important in your life. Use it to define goals and purpose for your service.

Don't get caught up in writing an essay packed with lofty goals. Aim to jot down a short, highly personal statement that guides you as a volunteer.

In the statement, include who you minister to, why you love this service, and what you find important about it. As you think, pay attention to thoughts that come to mind about these conditions.

- *The purpose of your service*
- *How you work to serve others*
- *How your God-given talents and personality factor into your service*
- *What you would love to achieve in ministry*
- *Why those goals matter to you*

Don't be afraid to aim high. Consider a favorite quote that comforts me in many situations: "Shoot for the moon. Even if you miss, you'll still land among the stars."

Truthfully, my philosophy is simple. I want to use the creative gifts God has given me to eternally impact students and leaders through the knowledge that they are forgiven, loved, and accepted through Jesus.

Section 2

This means I want my students to know how dearly Jesus loves them. I want them to understand what He meant when He promised to give us abundant life (John 10:10). I want them to feel accepted just as they are and comforted by the knowledge that they're children of our God, who freely loves and forgives them through the sacrifice of Jesus on the cross. I want grace and knowledge to permeate every area of their lives as they navigate adolescence and adulthood. I want them to have an honest, open relationship with their Savior.

I value using creativity to reach my students with these profound truths. I constantly seek to teach in every experience, activity, joy, and defeat in my daily adventures with students. My faith is alive and woven through every thread of my life. I love openly sharing the narrative of God working in my life so my students start to see God working in theirs too.

In my philosophy of ministry, I focused on a Bible verse that really speaks to me. In fact, 2 Timothy 1:7 is inscribed on a bracelet I wear almost every day: "For God gave us a spirit not of fear but of power and love and self-control."

Unfortunately, that admonition for self-discipline rarely works when I grumpily reach for a second cup of coffee in the morning.

Still, in the years spent working with leaders, I find it fascinating to see that God's living and active Word never fails. It always accomplishes His purposes (Isaiah 55:11).

The Word connects with individual Christians in powerful ways. Some of the wisest and most humble leaders I know resonate with verses of comfort, while others choose verses about trust or strength to encourage them.

Take a look at verses that tug at your heart, and see if you recognize a common theme in them. Perhaps it's a message about taking a step of faith or acting with courage. Maybe you connect with God's words to the downcast and disheartened, or feel uplifted by Jesus' words to care for the needy.

Examining the Scripture that speaks to you can give you insight about who and what you feel passionate about.

I can't tell you how many times I jotted something down on a note and stuck it to my fridge or bathroom mirror. Trust me, I need that smack in the noggin every day. I bet you do too. Stick notes with your favorite verses at places you'll see them every day.

And once you finish ironing out your philosophy statement, write it on a note and tape it to your mirror. Let it guide you daily, and let it serve as a much-needed reminder as to why you matter in God's kingdom.

Tackle goals next. I encourage you to write weekly goals, quarterly goals, and yearly goals for your life.

Whether you're a stay-at-home parent, a high school student, or a high-level executive, you can benefit from setting personal goals and priorities. No matter your age, experience level, educational background, or role, identifying goals you want to accomplish gives a sense of direction, purpose, and satisfaction.

Include your volunteer commitments, personal interests, professional ambitions, and spiritual objectives. Make sure your goals show a healthy mix of personal and professional aspirations, to balance you. Don't worry about getting overly detailed by scheduling every day of the year with meticulous notes. And be realistic. Going from King Couch Potato to climbing Mount Everest in six months probably isn't achievable.

Setting basic goals can help cut out extraneous efforts and save time in the long run. (Why do you spend valuable time and money collecting toothpicks, anyway?) Instead, highlight activities you feel passionate about and that utilize your God-given personality and talents.

To do:

Find video clip
Review lesson
~~Crawl back into bed~~
Buy snacks, craft supplies,
COFFEE
~~Invest in coffee futures~~
Talk to pastor about Jamie
~~Avoid Jamie's parents~~
Call Jamie's parents
Recruit volunteers to paint
youth room
Find retreat location
~~Update resumé~~

What do you do first?

Covered in paint, my arms aching, I repeated one simple word over and over: "Help."

I raced against the clock, frantically trying to finish a massive youth facility remodel. I couldn't think straight. I had painted and moved furniture for hours. Every inch of my body ached. My brain flatlined and my willpower zapped into nothingness. All I could do was mutter a one-word prayer to God, trusting He knew exactly what I felt even if I couldn't put it into words.

I know you've been there too, in moments when all you can do is offer up a whisper of prayer.

Now that you spent some time understanding yourself as a leader, defined your goals (personal philosophy of ministry), and identified the necessary mind-set to guide you, it's time to figure out what to do first.

Always, the first thing to do is to pray, even if you just say one word. You may not necessarily spend an hour in deep prayer. Your head might feel so muddled that all you can squeak out is "Help me, God!" After all, it's difficult to fall down when you're already on your knees.

Concentrate on working on what's directly in front of you. Do you need to rein in a class of screaming three-year-olds and channel their energy into something positive? Then do that, and don't worry about rewriting the mission and vision of your children's ministry program at that moment.

Do you need to build relationships with a bunch of surly high schoolers who watched leaders come and go for years? Then work on connecting with them and gaining their trust rather than concentrating on all the other details of your role.

In my experience, it's far more terrifying to worry about starting than what actually happens when you dive right in. Like jumping into the ocean, once you get past the initial fears of deep water, sea creatures, and temperature, you find that the water isn't so bad after all. It's pretty fun. And yes, those waves are going to hit you every once in a while, but you'll manage to continue swimming along.

When prioritizing, people take precedence over tasks. To figure out where to spend your time, always choose working with people over crossing items off a to-do list. If that means it takes a few more weeks to figure out exactly which curriculum you want or you must wait to clean that messy Sunday School supply closet, so be it. You won't lie on you deathbed wishing you had spent more time organizing files rather than laughing and learning beside people.

Focus on the big picture of why you serve—to bless the people around you. Don't sweat the minute details too often. Will anyone else care that your desk drawer looks like an atom bomb went off? Probably not. They care about you genuinely caring for them at a time when they desperately need it.

Trust that the Holy Spirit will guide you step-by-step, even if you don't exactly know where to go. As one of my mentors, Christine, once told me, "Sometimes God lights the path just in time for you to step out onto it." Know you don't carry the weight of the world on your shoulders. You just serve out the role God called you to perform right now, at this particular moment in history, with the people He placed around you.

Though it may seem cheesy, remember to smile as you serve. You always have an opportunity to learn from every situation, good or bad. This knowledge will craft you into a one-of-a-kind masterpiece who can leave a mark on the world in a way that no one else can.

Support and serve with others

*The occasion inevitably will arise when
you're compelled to support something, even
though you personally disagree with it.*

In my case, it was the fateful Day of a Thousand Cookies.

A few years ago, my youth group challenged themselves to reach out to the community in a unique way. For reasons unknown to me, they settled on doing something kind for the people who camped out in store lines Thanksgiving night to get doorbuster deals in the wee hours of Black Friday.

In our community, thousands of people camped out in the cold nighttime hours. The youth planned to hit several major stores and serve hot chocolate and fresh-baked cookies to as many people as they could.

To top off an already grand plan, they also plotted to bring instruments and perform Christmas carols with great gusto. They wanted to witness about Jesus as they waited in the dark.

Ever the practical youth leader, I gently tried to reason with my eager students. "That's a lot of people to bake cookies for," I repeated a few dozen times to deaf ears. My overzealous teens would have none of my rational advice. Instead, they plowed ahead, buying huge amounts of cookie dough and hot chocolate mix in anticipation of feeding thousands.

Internally, I could only think of how doomed the entire operation seemed.

Despite reservations, I encouraged the youth. Despite my chagrin, I spoke kindly of their operation to parents, co-workers, and friends. And I spent an entire day literally slaving over a hot oven with my teens, baking over fifteen hundred cookies. Even now, I can recall the steaming kitchen and the clank of metal trays whizzing in and out of the oven. I remember the painful assembly line of blistered fingers that tied the cookies in individual bags and knotted a cheerful little bow on each.

Though I often wanted to throw my spatula in the air and flounce out of the kitchen in exhaustion, I persevered. And though our efforts with the Black Friday crowds weren't perfect by any stretch of the imagination, we still handed out all of our cookies and gallons of hot chocolate.

Our community was touched by the creative effort of our teens, and we shared our faith with many strangers curious to know what compelled our actions. We had a great time! In fact, that tradition continues to this day, carried out by the same teens and leaders who started it years ago.

Any experience working with others provides opportunity for frustration and disagreement. Different personalities and backgrounds color our views of how ministry happens. We have varying ideas about how individuals should perform duties. How you handle the inevitable clash speaks volumes about the true nature of your character.

Whether you disagree with a small decision, like choosing to bake thousands of cookies for strangers, or oppose a huge issue, like the philosophy of your company, leaders must handle conflict in a Christian manner. After all, many eyes curiously watch you to see if your "walk matches the talk." In these moments, those around you see if the Gospel truly matters in your life.

One of the most underrated acts in society involves offering candid encouragement to one another. I'm not sure if the shortage of cheerful words comes from busy schedules, increasing detachment from face-to-face interactions, or worsening social skills, but people seem starved for even the smallest sliver of kindness today.

Hebrews 10:23–25 tells us, "Let us hold fast the confession of our hope without wavering, for He who promised is faithful. And let us consider how to stir up one another to love and good works, not neglecting to meet together, as is the habit of some, but encouraging one another, and all the more as you see the Day drawing near."

I worked retail for about a year in a popular clothing store. Dealing with hundreds of customers a day in our busy store gave me a firsthand glimpse into how harried and depressed a majority of people seem. I discovered how an honest compliment or short conversation can profoundly impact someone. While working at this store, I made it a personal mission to find something positive to say to every customer I talked to.

This challenge became something that actually blessed me in return. Customers opened up to me about all sorts of issues, and I saw firsthand the truth of Proverbs 12:25, "Anxiety in a man's heart weighs him down, but a good word makes him glad."

I eventually had to let my manager in on my personal crusade after she walked in on the second customer of the day crying in the fitting room and unloading a tragic story on me, the apparent fitting-room counselor.

After I stopped working retail, I shifted my challenge to make someone else smile every single day. Whether it's a cashier, co-worker, or student, I consider this mission of sharing joy to be one of the most important deeds I do in my life. It has also curbed me from making a hasty comment about someone's actions, decisions, or plans when I disagreed with him or her.

Supporting others means putting yourself second, after those you seek to serve. It's a hard thing to do, not something that comes naturally to us sinful folk. Sometimes you don't want the music to be so loud and so hip, but if it's reaching others for Christ and touching their hearts in a meaningful way, isn't that what really matters?

Section 2

Leaders in our organizations, churches, schools, and groups must show adaptability. Life requires growth and adjustment to change on a constant basis. Don't passively stick your head in the sand and insist that everything remain exactly the way you like it. That's selfish.

On the other hand, don't embrace change just for the sake of trying something new or being bold. As a wise person once said, "Don't be so open-minded that your brains fall out."

Honestly assess and embrace changes and challenges alike. Every experience offers a rich opportunity to learn. Stagnation is a poor option and a big pitfall.

Being a leader means supporting others, even when you disagree with them. Practice wisdom with your words. Give constructive criticism and honest feedback. Avoid adding fuel to needless fires.

Communicate with co-workers, staff, parents, and bosses frequently and openly. Share your victories and joys as well as frustrations. Your support matters. Your words of encouragement make a difference to leaders, students, and ministries. Choose to use your words to bless, not distress.

Pastors often tell me they feel thankful for leaders, a sentiment often voiced by my husband, Tyler. He's been a valuable source of encouragement for many leaders and me over the years. He says, "Leaders are the lifeblood of the Church, the essence of what makes a church go. I'm always aware of the sacrifices they make. They are the boots on the ground with kids and their families."

Remember that your pastors and ministry leaders are human too, and they feel the weight of discouragement just like everyone else. Often, they receive much more than their fair share of criticism.

As the wife of a pastor, I'm constantly shocked by how many well-meaning people take it upon themselves to deflate the pastor as they walk out the door from worship. Ironically, people don't nitpick a doctor or lawyer to the level of scrutiny they regularly inflict on church workers. Even small comments sting, such as "Oh, that sermon was much better than last week!" Choose instead to share positive, constructive words with those around you.

One important thing to note: your ministry leaders want to hear directly from you. "If you have complaints, don't be a 'parking lot complainer' and share them with others in the parking lot after an event," says Tyler. "Instead, share them directly with someone who can do something about it."

God has given each of us different passions and personalities. We're charged to use these gifts to guide others to faith in Jesus Christ. A mix of diverse people benefits any healthy organization, so embrace those different from you. Use your strengths to support others, and remember that you are an essential part of God's kingdom. By putting ministry first, above personal preferences, you show that you value the mission over your own ego.

In Tyler's opinion, leaders have much to offer their pastors and organization leaders. "It's important for volunteers to remember that you're driving toward the same goal," he told me. "You can very easily undermine the whole ministry if you let your agenda or bias take priority. If you seek to edify your own ministry at the expense of others, it can be detrimental overall. Be dedicated to pursuing God's will, viewing it not as an obligation but an opportunity. Create a positive atmosphere through a positive attitude."

In moments when you feel frazzled beyond belief, like when I discovered a week-old tray of cookie dough balanced precariously on top of a high shelf only one of my high schoolers could reach, remember that this, too, is part of the journey.

Be patient and allow God to teach you in the good times and bad. He is your mainstay, whatever path you traverse, and no matter how many frustrating things come your way. Concentrate on doing the job God laid before you and doing it to the best of your ability.

Nurture and support families

My brother and I reveled in a particularly unique game of bloody knuckles.

We played in complete silence, quietly biting back our exclamations of pain. We dared not scream because of where we played—in a church pew.

Growing up, our family went to church every Sunday, and our parents expected us to pay attention to the sermon. My brother and I occasionally sneaked a game of knuckle bruising while our parents listened intently to the pastor.

But another family practice taught us to forgo our game and focus on the message. You see, without fail, our family went out to lunch at a local café after church. As we ate, we discussed the sermon. Woe to us if we didn't contribute!

Some of my favorite memories involve our little family of four sitting around the table, debating and dissecting topics of faith, religion, and culture. Though I attended Lutheran schools my entire life, the formative foundation of my faith came from my parents actively discussing their own spiritual lives so openly.

Scripture tells us that God intended the family to serve as the foundation to teach children about life and faith. What happens in the formative years of a child's life echoes with eternal impact. "Train up a child in the way he should go; even when he is old he will not depart from it" (Proverbs 22:6).

Our families influence nearly every single part of our lives through positive or negative experiences. They hone our personalities, develop our habits, and influence our thought processes and attitudes. Many books have been written about the fact that families are simultaneously the greatest source of happiness and frustration in a person's life. As Charles Swindoll once said, "A family is a place where principles are hammered and honed on the anvil of everyday living."

With a healthy marriage, a robust family forms. Strong families create sound communities. Thriving communities form the foundation of our nation. And as we know, our nation contributes to history.

Unfortunately, we face a decline in stable settings for children and healthy families at this point in history.

Children navigate complicated webs of relationships at home. They may live in multiple homes on different days with shared-custody parents, stepparents, stepsiblings, half-siblings, grandparents, and extended family members. Many children struggle to relate to their parents' dates or live-in partners. Increasing numbers of grandparents raise young children when parents

American household size
Total households: 124,587,000

Family
Demographics

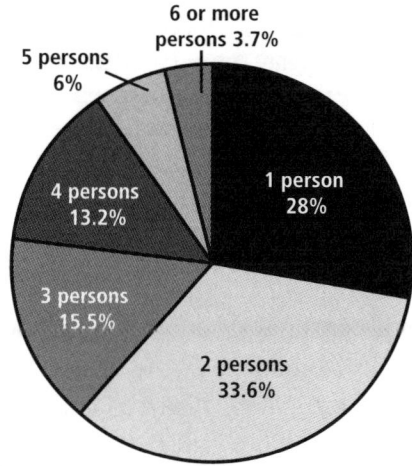

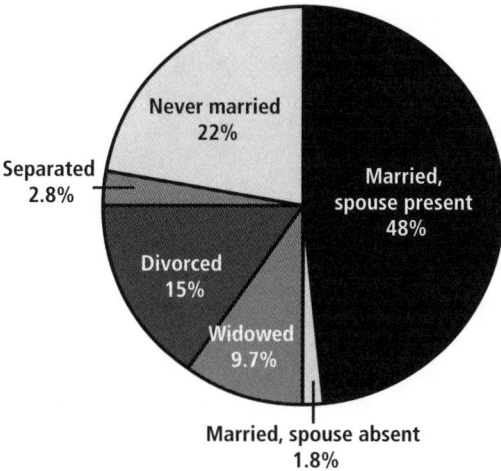

American household size pie chart:
- 6 or more persons 3.7%
- 5 persons 6%
- 4 persons 13.2%
- 3 persons 15.5%
- 2 persons 33.6%
- 1 person 28%

Marital status of American households
- Never married 22%
- Separated 2.8%
- Divorced 15%
- Widowed 9.7%
- Married, spouse present 48%
- Married, spouse absent 1.8%

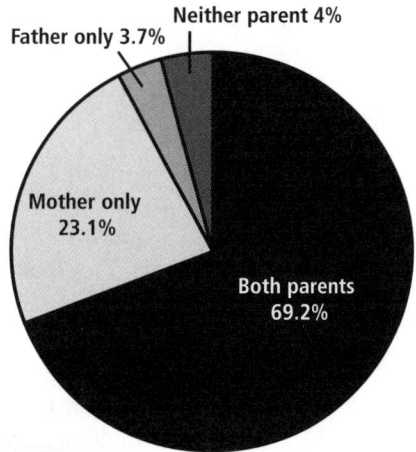

American households: With whom do children live?

With whom do children live pie chart:
- Neither parent 4%
- Father only 3.7%
- Mother only 23.1%
- Both parents 69.2%

SOURCE: US Census Bureau, Current Population Survey, 2015 Annual Social and Economic Supplement
www.census.gov

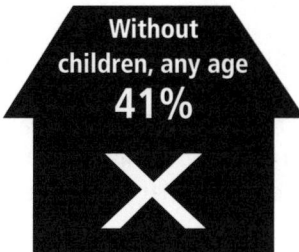

With children, any age 59%

Without children, any age 41%

American households with children

Art © Shutterstock, Inc.

cannot. Children may also experience a wider diversity of household types in their friends' homes than ever before.

Historically, the home offered academic and spiritual education, socialization, and recreation. Parents spent the majority of their time with their kids, working as well as playing and learning together. This time together allowed families to easily pass their values and traditions to future generations.

Today, schools, governments, and service agencies handle many socialization skills. Children receive education in schools and universities. Leagues, clubs, and community centers offer social and recreational events. Churches provide religious instruction. Strangers deliver medical care.

Our churches and ministries have unique opportunities to positively impact kids and their families. We should offer families the tools and skills to be healthy, productive centers of spiritual and personal development.

Unfortunately, many of our ministries and organizations work against families, often in subtle ways. Some systems encourage parents to drop off and pick up their kids without actually knowing what they learned. Some churches separate children and adults for all activities, including worship. Others schedule events that conflict with families' limited time together. Many good leaders unintentionally create closed-off clubs, with parents and siblings kept at arm's length and discouraged from involvement.

We must assess exactly what we're doing to invest in creating healthy opportunities for our families. Being a well-rounded leader means involving the entire family unit in whatever you do.

I witnessed firsthand the great value of including people of all ages, backgrounds, experiences, and generations together in activities and experiences. It's not difficult, but it requires intentional effort on our part.

Instrumental to this effort is understanding our role to equip families as the spiritual centers of faith. This means discipling and educating both students and their parents or guardians. Many parents feel clueless and unsupported as they raise their kids. This makes them more willing to chuck the responsibility our way. We must encourage and provide resources for these individuals. After all, they spend even more time handling these goofy kids than we do.

One important thing we can do is create opportunities for parents and kids to learn alongside one another. Families can serve the homeless together, team-teach Vacation Bible School, or discuss experiences after a lesson or a trip.

Recently, I helped with an outreach effort where entire families handed out hot dogs to hungry soccer fans. Grandmas grilled and wrapped food. Parents shuttled wrapped hot dogs to the kids, who walked all over the parking lot to hand them out. Instead of just involving our youth, we gave entire families a chance to laugh and grow together. They inspired one another to serve the community.

Instead of creating a closed culture where we minister only to specific age groups, we can use our position to connect with several people in a family.

Research says children and adolescents appreciate and respond to a wide range of adults. So, invite people of all ages to get involved in your ministries, and don't just plug in parents as last-minute chaperones for a late-night lock-in. Give grandparents, aunts and uncles, and older siblings opportunities to participate in your mission too. Their wisdom and experience add valuable contributions.

Choose your words carefully and speak positive words about parents. Our words carry weight with the children who look up to us and with teenagers who feel that they can confide in us. Talk about the importance of forgiveness and love in a family. Speak often your intention to partner with parents and families to raise children. They're not alone; you're in it together.

Helping equip the entire family means emphasizing a life of regular spiritual practices. We can teach and model family prayer and devotional time, participation in regular worship and in the church community, service, and tithing.

Provide resources for a variety of needs. Keep a file of helpful pamphlets and articles on a variety of subjects. Make a list of counseling centers, women's shelters, support groups, and websites so you don't have to dig around when troubled adults come to you at wits' end. Strive to be a friendly and informative leader for the families. Make an effort to connect with younger siblings, cousins, grandparents, aunts and uncles, and friends.

Know that frazzled parents or guardians sometimes just need someone else to talk to about their children. Maintaining an open and disarming attitude can provide a lifeline of encouragement to individuals who need to vent without feeling judged.

Communicate clearly and often about activities and concerns of your ministry or organization. As I like to tell my co-workers, "When in doubt, overcommunicate."

As you plan activities, consider the busy schedules of today's families. Typically, the beginning and end of the school year, Thanksgiving, and Christmas rank among the most stressful times of the year for families. Avoid planning events that draw kids away from their families during these times, however good your intentions.

Do your best to accommodate parents getting to and from work. Avoid interrupting dinnertime. Consider condensing or eliminating pointless meetings, and do something creative and refreshing instead. For instance, my church started nixing information meetings for youth ministry events and instead emails short videos to families to watch together at home.

As Psalm 103:17–18 reminds us, "But the steadfast love of the LORD is from everlasting to everlasting on those who fear Him, and His righteousness

Section 2

to children's children, to those who keep His covenant and remember to do His commandments."

By uniting with families to influence children and youth positively, we invest in supporting each generation and their relationship with Christ. We build a strong foundation for the future Church.

Set up safe practices

I learned the hard way that four students can sneak kisses in the time it takes me to brush my teeth.

That's why I like to point out one rule you absolutely cannot break when you work with kids.

Never, ever leave the kids alone. Not even for a second.

I know you're thinking, "Not my students—they're sweethearts. They wouldn't get in trouble in the time it takes me to swing by the supply closet and grab another pack of paper. They're angels."

Let me tell you precisely how my angels taught me this cardinal rule.

We stopped for the night after a long drive across country on a mission trip with a gaggle of teenagers. My wiped-out fellow leaders fell asleep promptly. As the only adult still awake, I knew I had to keep an eye on the handful of teens still rustling around, brushing their teeth.

Unfortunately, I decided to slip away for a brief moment to brush my teeth too.

In the few minutes I left my youth unsupervised, they managed to set up a game of spin the bottle. Two students were heartily engaged in a kiss when I arrived back in the room.

Granted, they all had fresh breath at that point.

If you ever find yourself as the sole leader in a room, figure out how to get what you need without leaving your kids unattended. That might mean sending a pair of kids down the hall to grab supplies, scheduling a brief break in your day with another adult, or grabbing a passing parent to help you out for a few minutes. Figure out what helps you.

This leads me to an even more important point: do everything you can to safeguard your ministry or organization.

As volunteers and leaders, our role is a delicate mix of leadership, wisdom, encouragement, and fun. But above all, we are responsible for the well-being of other human lives. And let's face it, most of the humans we serve don't always make good decisions for themselves.

As a primary strategy, set up a healthy and practical ratio of adults to kids that keeps leaders and students safe. Whenever possible, schedule two adults to lead at all times. Never let leaders meet one-on-one with a student behind closed doors. If leaders end up alone with one student, tell them to prop the door open and stand in the doorframe. Leaders should never be alone with a student in a vehicle if they can help it.

Section 2

For overnight events or trips, I recommend that leaders maintain strict privacy, especially when it comes to changing their clothes and bathing. Leaders should never change their shirts in front of same-gender students. They should not share beds or pillows or even snuggle under the same blanket. I also advise against sharing personal items of any sort, such as lip balm, soap, toothbrushes, and water bottles.

Many leaders ask about appropriate behavior when it comes to touching students, from hugs to headlocks. This is a tricky subject, and there's no exact guideline. Unfortunately, the world we live in is one rife with suspicion, and for good reason. Each week, we read a new story about a trusted teacher, coach, or parent perpetrating some disturbing behavior on innocent children.

You must be diligent for the sake of the youth and everyone who faithfully serves with good intentions. Ministry already struggles to identify and exempt those who prey on children. As a leader, you must act with maturity and protect your ministry so that kids' minds don't even wander in a perverted direction with you.

Leaders bear the responsibility to help each person safeguard our roles with children by acting above reproach. My advice? Don't initiate any physical contact with a student, and use wary caution when students try to initiate with you. Don't play with a kid's hair, playfully put a student in a choke hold, pick them up, give piggyback rides, give massages, pet their head, let them sit on your lap, or let them share a chair with you.

When kids feel upset, many instinctively reach out for someone to hold them. In that case, and only when a student expressly asks for physical comfort, it is appropriate to hug them back. Even so, I encourage you to offer your students a "side-hug," if possible. You never want to be a source of temptation or confusion in emotionally charged situations with kids.

All adults over the age of eighteen who work with minors need to pass a background check. Check with your particular state, organization, and insurance company for specifics. For the safety of the youth and their families, follow insurance requirements and exceed them when you can.

Adults who drive students off campus also must undergo background checks and have copies of their driver's licenses on file. Drivers must carry signed permission forms for every single child.

If you plan to travel out of your region, get medical information for every person, including adults. Keep a copy with you and give drivers the forms with other permission slips. Although hospitals still may not treat minors without parental permission, having insurance information and contact numbers in one place makes it easier to proceed. Again, consult your organization's insurance provider or state agency for guidelines that often change.

If a student gets injured at an event or while in your care, write an incident report and immediately share it with the child's guardians. In fact, it's wise to document many things regarding the kids in your care, such as bullying, disciplinary issues, and incidents of anger or confrontation.

Additionally, most state laws list paid and unpaid people who take full or intermittent responsibility for children, youth, and the elderly as mandated reporters. This means the law requires you to report reasonable suspicions of abuse.

If you suspect a child or teenager is being harmed emotionally or physically or is being neglected, you are legally bound to report it to the proper authorities, usually a local child protection agency. Failure to report suspected abuse could make you and your organization morally and financially liable. Check your state laws to make sure exactly where you stand.

Overwhelmed?

Yeah, sometimes it seems like a lot to take in.

Unfortunately, we must adopt this mind-set in order to maintain the safety of our students and our leaders. In a world racked with countless stories of adults abusing children and teens, a whispered rumor can undo an entire organization. In this lawsuit-happy climate, rumors can cause unimaginable damage to reputations of individuals and organizations.

By working proactively to make our programs and ministries above reproach, we can instill a deep sense of trust and confidence in our programs with our community.

If someone sues, you will need to prove in a court of law that you made reasonable attempts to protect the individuals in your charge. Even if your intent is to host a carefree, unstructured activity or club, you're still responsible for the well-being of the people around you. That requires you to use your brain and carefully think through the decisions you make about events and activities.

Bungee jumping off the church roof into a pool filled with whipped cream? Probably not a good bet. And also a horrible waste of perfectly good whipped cream.

Years ago, a teenager did an impersonation of me in front of my youth group. He coined the phrase "Cassie the Fun Stopper" and mimicked me supervising a rowdy group with a clipboard full of waivers in my hands, saying things like "Don't do something I'll make you regret."

Hey, you know what they say, right? They tease you because they like you.

While the joke was all in fun, there's some truth to this perception.

For students' safety, I ask them to sign in for every activity and list an emergency contact number. I keep that information in an easily accessible place for all leaders, ideally near a door so you can grab quickly. Could I just have an emergency form for each person on my computer and be fine? Yes, but having students sign in for every event provides an accurate number that we can immediately access in case of a chaotic situation. It also serves as an easy-to-reach log of student names and information for every leader in case I become incapacitated and unable to get to it myself.

Unfortunately, we never know when tragedies may strike. It's imperative that we carefully think through our roles and determine in advance how to remain safe. We also need to know how to react when things go wrong.

Once, in the middle of a lock-in with nearly one hundred teenage girls, I discovered a suspicious-looking man attempting to break into our facility. Immediately, I locked all the doors, pulled the blinds down, moved kids away from the windows into the center of the room, and called the police.

Ultimately, the man disappeared and no harm came to us. But the event jarringly reminded me to remain vigilant. The safety of my students comes first, even if others think I go overboard with preparations and procedures.

When we protect the precious children God entrusted to us, we demonstrate a positive witness of responsibility and safety to a whole new generation.

Make emergency plans

"STAY THERE! YOU'LL BE JUST FINE!" I yelled into my phone as it buzzed again with another incoming call.

My co-leaders shot looks of desperation as they simultaneously shouted the same instructions into their phones.

What started out as a pleasant youth group outing to a giant theme park turned into every youth leader's nightmare. An ominous thunderstorm quickly rolled over us. Lightning nearly struck the tall buildings surrounding us. Windows shook with overpowering thunder and forceful rain.

Our group of teenagers scattered like cockroaches in a kitchen. Kids hurriedly ducked for cover in different buildings. Separated from the group, they naturally panicked.

I stood with two co-leaders inside a crowded restaurant, soaked to the skin, fielding call after call from terrified teens. They felt confused. They felt scared. They didn't know what to do. They wanted to find us.

In moments of extreme tension, our heart rates soar and minds become clouded. That day, the simple solution of waiting out the storm and eventually reconnecting with the rest of the group didn't occur to our youth. Paralyzed, they couldn't reason coherently. They needed a calm leader to give them confident and quick step-by-step instructions.

Often, leaders are lax in thinking through the worst-case scenarios we could face with kids in our care. Watching shootings and accidents on the news, we lull ourselves into a state of complacency, thinking it could never happen to us.

In reality, minor and major emergencies happen frequently. Kids hear the news too, and many of them fear such tragedies striking them. Taking measures to protect your students comforts them and shows them how deeply you value them.

Depending on your location and role, you may encounter many types of emergencies. Perhaps your threat is weather related, with the possibility of a tornado, earthquake, violent thunder- or windstorm, or flood. On the other hand, you could face a fire, toxic gas, or a chemical spill. Perhaps your biggest threats are poisonous snakes or other animals, and you need to prepare for those dangers. Of course, everyone needs to safeguard against sexual predators and violent offenders.

It's important to work through emergency plans carefully in advance. Because most people don't think clearly and logically in the middle of an emergency, it's vital to prepare crisis plans when we can think calmly, thoroughly, and thoughtfully. Even first responders, such as police, firemen, and military, rely heavily on role-playing these same types of stressful circumstances.

Quite simply, I always start with one question: What's the absolute worst-case scenario in this instance? Then I begin listing actions and procedures.

In my mind, I play out every possible horrific emergency we might encounter. I envision my youth facility on fire, a crazed madman breaking into our Vacation Bible School, and a burglar attempting to steal my computer while I lead a children's event. I envision watching a tornado destroy our building and an epidemic hitting our kids during a lock-in.

Don't let these various scenarios upset you. Instead, carefully note things that demand attention. In the grips of a highly charged emotional moment, you won't hold a checklist to remember exactly what to do.

Your emergency action plan should always include an evacuation policy and procedure, including a floor plan to help direct people. Always know your current address and location. Decide how to communicate with others. Keep phone numbers of contacts immediately accessible, including parents and emergency services. Keep a fully stocked first-aid kit within easy reach, not locked away in a cabinet on the highest shelf in the room. Know the exact number of people in your group at any given moment.

In a difficult situation, others will watch you closely. If you panic because you didn't adequately prepare your space, plans, or mind, your terror will infect the people around you. However, if you thought through a variety of different scenarios and prepared adequately, you can snap into action quickly when needed.

Also consider the kinds of supplies you need.

Let's say a bad storm knocked out power to your building. Do you have flashlights handy and a way to call for help? Phone land lines become unavailable if the electricity goes out. Weather can affect cell phone towers. What about handling an accidental poisoning of a small child or a serious injury? Thinking through these scenarios, developing action plans, and stocking tools you need all make the difference between successfully managing a crisis and coping with a terrible tragedy.

Recently, I camped overnight in a church with a group of teenagers. Unbeknownst to me, someone from our group blew out the pilot lights on the giant church stove. Gas slowly leaked into the building for several hours. By the time we smelled the gas, it was in the early hours of the morning.

Because our leadership team prepared an emergency plan, we evacuated our entire group to the parking lot in under a minute. We called the fire department without hesitation and let them know our exact location, an unfamiliar place for us. In fact, we snapped into action so quickly that all our sleep-befuddled teenagers could say was, "Why are we all so calm right now? It's the middle of the night and our building might explode."

Don't worry, everyone survived. No one blew up.

Let's summarize practical ways to safeguard your people and ministry.

Know your surroundings.

Have a good working knowledge of your location, including emergency exits, bathrooms, and safe places to hide in a pinch. Know the address and phone number of your building too. Know what various alarms in the community and the facility mean. Know how to use the phone. Often, church or business phones require you to dial nine first to get an outside line.

Stock a first-aid kit.

Keep your first-aid kit in a nearby secure place. Make it portable if you can. Add a flashlight and a whistle too, handy items to grab if you quickly need to evacuate a room.

Have an emergency plan.

Develop actions and procedures for emergency situations. Teach emergency plans to other leaders. In a difficult situation, leaders need to work together for the good of the whole group.

Keep your phone close.

Most people have a cell phone, but intentionally keep it on your body while you work with others. Also, keep it charged so it doesn't falter in the middle of a life-or-death situation.

Program emergency numbers into your phone ahead of time. Besides 911, add the local police station, poison control, and the fire department in the favorites section of your phone. Post copies of these and other important phone numbers near phones in public areas of your facility. In the chaos of an emergency, you don't want to scramble to call for help.

Count heads and have numbers handy.

Know the exact number of people in your group at all times. A good leader constantly counts and recounts. If caught in a crisis, make sure to count and track students carefully. Use the emergency contact numbers from the sign-in sheet in case you need to call parents or guardians.

Be confident in prayer.

In the middle of a tense situation, leaders may feel alone. But you are not alone! You are in the hands of God Almighty, the Creator of the universe. No matter what happens, you and your students can always pray. Let God's perfect peace guard your hearts and your minds, even in the most stressful circumstances.

Art © Shutterstock, Inc.

Section 2

Regardless of age, people process emergencies, disasters, and crisis situations differently. People reel from direct involvement, worry about family and friends, or panic. Some feel numb, shocked, or afraid. Others immediately feel horror or anger. Still others feel frustrated or helpless because they can't do more to fix a situation.

As a leader, you have the ability to greatly impact people in these situations. Help guide through practical actions, such as finding a safe space to hunker down, providing first aid, leading prayer, and sharing comfort.

Kids often struggle to express their feelings, so they often distract themselves to avoid feeling upset. It's important to allow people time to process the event and not push for immediate feedback. Encourage people to express their emotions. Provide a safe outlet for sharing strong feelings. Share your own honest reactions of feeling scared, helpless, or stressed out. Reassure others and recommend clinging to Jesus and confiding feelings to Him.

Emergencies can provide youth with chances to grow and learn new things about themselves. They can give them a maturity others may not possess. A crisis can have a positive outcome and give us a glimpse of our strength and loving concern for one another and our community.

Ultimately, work hard to set up a safe and secure ministry and develop an emergency plan. Don't wait around for someone else to do it or for something to happen first.

As they say in sports, the best defense is a strong offense.

Avoid self-sabotage (single-handed destruction of your own efforts)

I've had my fair share of moments when I wanted to throttle a kid for doing something stupid. One instance stands out in particular, the time a student took a swan dive onto a couch and cracked it in half.

Oh, did I mention it was a very expensive, very new leather couch that didn't even belong to me?

This particular student was one of the zaniest youths I ever had the pleasure of teaching. He simultaneously brought smiles to our faces while striking fear in our hearts as leaders.

The absolute definition of a goofball, he did everything he could dream up to press my buttons. If I held up an apple as an object lesson, he grabbed it and bit into it before I snatched it back. If I stood up to give devotions, he stole the microphone and started singing. Other youth leaders actually refused to sit next to him in church because he never stopped disrupting people around him. The innocents stifled their reactions so vigorously that they often became red-faced and silently heaved with laughter through sermons.

By the Laws of Youth Ministry, kids who give you the biggest disciplinary headaches tend to stick around longest. In this student's case, he became an amazing young man I'm proud to call a friend today. But let me tell you, that certainly was not the case when he was in high school and decided to ratchet up the intensity of his mischievousness.

While I was sitting with my high schoolers and leafing through a stack of papers, my troublemaker got bored. Ever the showman, he decided to break the ice in dramatic fashion.

Behind my back, he slowly sneaked up to the back of the couch. He tentatively stood up. As I turned to yell at him, he gleefully grinned and shouted, "Cannonball!" Then he threw himself onto the couch headfirst like an Olympic diver.

The couch promptly cracked and sagged, tumbling all of us into a disorderly heap in the middle.

I can laugh about this incident now. It helps to own up to the mistakes I made myself that fateful day. I failed to organize my lesson well and didn't pay enough attention to the kids. I allowed too much downtime, which made my students lose interest. Boredom led to the demise of our youth center couch.

Even so, we are not responsible for the choices our students make. Get that through your head. If you need to get it tattooed on your forearm to remind yourself of this fact frequently, do it.

Of course, if you work with middle schoolers, you probably have a tattoo already, an unsightly, unintelligible image inked on in permanent marker, courtesy of your students.

Setting up a safe and productive experience for the kids in our care falls on our shoulders. That means thinking through possible mistakes so furniture emerges unscathed. Knowing how to keep people safe is critical, but understanding how to get and keep the attention of kids and teens is key to your success too.

Sometimes it helps to understand what we do that can single-handedly sabotage our events. Leaders commonly stumble over these ten mistakes when working with kids and teens.

TEN: Solo act

All leaders need prayer and fellowship with others. Corporate worship is vital. So is accountability.

Many leaders naively carry the weight of the world, or at least their particular corner of ministry, all on their own. Remember, we all need others to broaden our perspectives, keep us on track when we skirt off the rails, and give us unclouded advice. Some of my dearest friends are partners in ministry living all across the country. They offer an endless source of encouragement to me.

Surround yourself with others to help support and uplift you. You will benefit greatly, as will your youth and other volunteers.

Research indicates that kids grow optimally with several significant adults actively involved in their lives. Don't limit the kids to see just you, but find others for them to interact with too.

Realistically, splitting responsibilities among a few people lightens the load and allows healthier ministries to grow and multiply.

NINE: Sloppy safety

Thoughtless or sloppy procedures eventually pay unwelcome dividends. As described in the previous sections, spend some time considering how you would handle various unexpected situations. Develop emergency procedures and standard practices that reflect preparation. List and collect supplies you need.

EIGHT: Refusing to discipline

Working with kids in any capacity requires leaders to provide discipline.

No matter how angelic your students seem, they're still maturing, which means they'll make mistakes often.

Adults guide students as they navigate the path to self-sufficiency and independence. Thus, correction is instrumental for their growth. By refusing to lovingly discipline students when needed, you stunt their growth and sabotage their ability to grow into well-rounded adults.

SEVEN: Never breaking the ice

Kids are like wild squirrels. They naturally distrust adults, and it takes a while until they can tolerate you, let alone eat out of your hand.

Don't expect to dive into soul-searching conversations without thawing out your kids first. Start your time together with fun icebreakers, games and activities, and discussion questions to ponder.

Asking something like "What's the biggest temptation in your life right now?" results in uncomfortable silence if you don't properly warm up your students first.

SIX: No plan B

Always make a backup plan.

One of the easiest ways to sabotage an event is to never consider what to do if everything falls apart. If you count on everything going exactly as planned, without interruptions, misbehaving kids, and faltering technology, you're living in a fantasy world.

In fact, things rarely go according to plan when working with kids. And if they do, you should be writing this book.

In my world, leaders mess up, technology fails, lessons fall flat, and kids lose interest. By accepting that plans sometimes need to change and jumping to a backup plan, you can salvage a flop. It's all about rolling with the punches. Sometimes this means taking advantage of an unplanned circumstance and making it into a teachable moment.

FIVE: Treating kids like babies

One of the biggest mistakes adults make with students is treating them like babies. Do kids still require boundaries, education, and assistance? Yes! But they're also developing their own beliefs, lifestyles, and personalities.

Colored by discord, kids warily weave their way through childhood and into the uncertain world of adulthood. We insult our students by treating them like little kids, speaking down to them, and demeaning them.

Instead, acknowledge this complex and confusing time in life. Openly respect these fledgling little adults. Remember that they aren't fully capable of independence quite yet, so your opinions matter in their eyes. By consistently challenging them to aim higher instead of babying them, you help youth feel accepted and understood.

FOUR: Unconcern about understanding

I hate to break it to you, but kids today grow up in a vastly different world than the one you grew up in.

Yes, students still typically deal with the same universal struggles kids have groaned about since time began. But this generation faces many unique pressures. Chances are high that you never experienced online bullying or had to deal with sexting fiascoes blowing up your school. Most kids wade through these issues themselves or with their friends daily.

As a leader, it's your duty to seek to understand this distinctive generation. Don't assume their experiences match yours as a teen, or that their classrooms operate the way yours did at their age.

Show genuine interest in their culture, and they'll open up to you. Good luck, though, remembering the names of all the YouTube stars they adore.

THREE: Lack of preparation

Failing to prepare derails youth events. If you wait until the time of the event to unwrap or organize supplies, set up the music playlist, or make copies, you are ensuring nothing but chaos and lost interest from your students.

Avoid this by putting effort into organizing your supplies before kids show up, including drinks, snacks, handouts, soccer balls, and crayons.

In the same way, prepare your leaders by sharing schedules, games, and activities and by choosing or assigning roles. Remind them that they serve a vital part in sharing God's love with others.

TWO: Nonexistent boundaries

A few months ago, I walked through Disney World with my family. As we traversed a bridge spanning a café on the bottom level, I watched two middle school boys lean over the railing and spit heartily onto people eating below.

Without thinking, I yelled at them. They turned and looked at me in horror as I stood my ground, shaking my finger and chewing them out. It didn't even cross my mind that they weren't my students or that they were with their own parents who obviously failed to discipline them. I just knew these two boys had stepped beyond my personal boundary for how kids should behave, and I had to deal with it. Immediately.

My family was completely embarrassed by the demonstration of a teacher's superb ability to discipline anyone at any time. (C'mon, it's a gift!) But it reminded me that boundaries and consequences for breaking them matter profoundly when dealing with kids.

Set your behavior limits early and stick to them. Enforce your expectations without emotion and do so equally with all of your students. Don't let the persistence of nagging kids change your boundaries for behavior in your classroom or youth group. Stick to your guns. They'll respect you for it.

ONE: Ignoring Jesus

The worst way to sabotage a youth event is to fail to share the Gospel of Jesus Christ. By filling time merely playing games or talking exclusively about social justice, pop culture, world news, or morality and ignoring the message of the cross, you do a disservice to your students.

Avoiding the Gospel message in favor of anything else is a flat failure for leaders.

Our children live in a world that constantly distracts them from this life-saving Gospel message. We must constantly remember our purpose: to point students to Jesus at all times and in all ways. They are hungry for this message. They yearn to question and discuss what their faith means to them.

Our students and we need to know that even in the worst of our mistakes and muddled lives, we are forgiven anew by the sacrifice of Jesus on our behalf. Our worth isn't measured in how flawlessly we execute an event or perfectly plan a lesson, but in our identities as sons and daughters of the King.

Even in our biggest failings, we can take comfort in the beautiful words of Psalm 103:8–12: "The LORD is merciful and gracious, slow to anger and abounding in steadfast love. He will not always chide, nor will He keep His anger forever. He does not deal with us according to our sins, nor repay us according to our iniquities. For as high as the heavens are above the earth, so great is His steadfast love toward those who fear Him; as far as the east is from the west, so far does He remove our transgressions from us."

Manage conflict and communicate with others

Stuffed a bully into a trash can? Yeah, I'm guilty.

Those who know me can tell you that I'm a tad on the feisty side.

Of course, my family would probably describe me quite differently, most likely using words like *strong-willed*, *stubborn*, and *headstrong*.

Personality traits like these landed me in a few fights as a teenager. Middle school, in particular, was a challenging time in my life. (Come on, no one actually liked middle school, right?)

The girls in my middle school class had a long history of cruelty to one another. As a tomboy, I mostly hung around with the boys at recess so I could play soccer, but I still frequently got sucked into the angst of my classmates. When my peers wouldn't listen to my pleas to leave one another alone, I quit talking and took a different approach.

I stuffed the biggest bully into a trash can.

Now, don't get me wrong. I don't advocate this as a solution to solve conflict. I merely use it to highlight the way I approached a disagreement and to show I've come a long way since then in understanding how to deal with discord.

Besides, if you try it now, you'll read this book from a cozy spot in your local jail.

Though safety and engagement take priority in our service, handling conflict also rises to the top of the leader list. Your personal approach to handling tension and disagreement doubtlessly comes into play. And whether you work for a school, club, team, or church, how you handle conflict either strengthens or tears down your organization. It's vital to understand how to handle conflict correctly, in a proper, level-headed manner.

Contrary to popular belief, conflict isn't bad; it merely shows action and growth taking place. It's a basic human need to feel understood and supported. However, people strive to meet these needs in many different ways. Often, these differences of lifestyle and opinion cause undue stress in our relationships with others. Tension tends to crop up over differences in ideas, goals, motivations, and values.

I learned firsthand that a little bit of conflict can sometimes be a good thing.

As a kid, I loved to jump wildly on an oversized trampoline in my backyard. I spent many long hours flipping head over heels, twisting, and trying out new moves.

My parents never stopped cautioning me about the risks I took. They reminded me frequently about the importance of remaining safe, not being reckless with my tricks, and never jumping alone without their supervision. Their nagging became an aggravating annoyance in my life.

Guess what? I sneaked outside one afternoon when they weren't home to jump all on my own.

And, gulp! I hid this story from them for years. Sorry, Mom and Dad.

As I attempted an impressive somersault, I misjudged and landed hard, directly on my neck. My body flopped down on the trampoline, and I found myself temporarily paralyzed. Since I was home alone, I could only lie there helplessly until I regained control of my limbs. Thank You, God, for no permanent damage!

In this instance, the desires of my parents to keep me safe conflicted with my desire to enjoy life. They just wanted me to survive to adulthood, at least. The opinions of both entities deserved consideration even though we disagreed.

The longer you serve as a volunteer, the more likely you'll encounter people who disagree with you. Despite your best attempts to get along and work together, conflict inevitably worms its way into your organization.

Diverse personalities deal with conflict differently. Some people minimize tension; others completely ignore it. Some compromise, trying to find a solution that works for everyone. Others resolutely hold firm, not budging an inch. Still other individuals love confrontation and engage in healthy problem-solving. Some tackle problems with aggression.

Pay attention to how you respond to conflict. If something minor strikes a major chord with you, it may signal a significant need in your life, such as a need to feel validated or safe. Talk with a trusted friend or a counselor to recognize and understand these personal flash points and develop ways to respond more confidently.

Properly understood, conflict can cause you to pause and reconsider, curtail a thoughtless plan, or recheck your motives. Ignoring tension causes conflicts to fester. If not addressed, conflict can fester from minor irritation into deep-seated frustration.

Our role as volunteers necessitates responding to conflict in a calm and rational way, without anger or resentment. Often, conflicts provide opportunity to grow personally as well as strengthen partnerships with others. Dealing with difficult situations builds confidence and trust in relationships. Strong relationships survive challenges and continue to grow. When you objectively analyze conflict and examine differences in a Christlike manner, you open the door to better teamwork, better relationships, and better long-term outcomes.

Make every effort to deal with problems in a loving and truthful manner. Continue to support other ministries verbally even if you feel personally frustrated with a situation. The way you handle conflict with a co-worker, parent, or student speaks untold volumes to the people around you about your leadership.

To deal with tension in a healthy manner, we need to address conflict head-on and talk first with the person at the source. Our attitude must be one of love, respect, and humbleness. We must focus comments carefully on behavior and events, not personalities. Seek to listen first. Physically hold your tongue with your fingers if you can't keep your mouth shut long enough to let someone else say their piece.

Discover common ground between you. Do your best to identify where you agree, not just where you disagree. Work to put together a plan to work on each conflict, and take steps to follow through with those ideas. Don't be tempted to brush an argument under the rug. And don't bad-mouth the person or situation to others.

Only after you have honestly exhausted every option to resolve the problem directly with the person should you attempt to bring anyone else into the situation. Do so only after prayer and thoughtful effort to deal with the tension in a godly manner.

Jesus gave us a great rubric for addressing conflict with other believers. He said, "If your brother sins against you, go and tell him his fault, between you and him alone. If he listens to you, you have gained your brother. But if he does not listen, take one or two others along with you, that every charge may be established by the evidence of two or three witnesses. If he refuses to listen to them, tell it to the church. And if he refuses to listen even to the church, let him be to you as a Gentile and a tax collector. Truly, I say to you, whatever you bind on earth shall be bound in heaven, and whatever you loose on earth shall be loosed in heaven. Again I say to you, if two of you agree on earth about anything they ask, it will be done for them by My Father in heaven. For where two or three are gathered in My name, there am I among them" (Matthew 18:15–20).

At a young age, I learned to tackle difficult situations with humor. My father modeled this behavior. He mastered the art of dealing with prickly circumstances with a smile and a deep laugh as he carefully joked about the issues at hand. Humor helps communicate challenging expressions without offending others, as long as you laugh with the other person and not at them.

How do you resolve conflict with a minimal amount of stress? Here are some tips that work for me.

DO

Choose battles wisely
Conflict = action, growth
Pause, reconsider
Value relationships
Listen first
Be calm, rational, assertive
Speak the truth in love
Focus on objective issues
Examine differences
Find common ground
Find agreement, make a plan, or agree to disagree
Forgive, move on
Build up

DON'T

Swat every fly
Conflict = problems, mistrust
Charge ahead
Value winning
Speak first
Be loud, irrational
Use anger, aggression
Focus on personalities
Maximize differences
Refuse to compromise
Avoid a plan
Blame
Hold grudges
Tear down

◆ *Choose battles wisely.*

Consider whether an issue is really worth the time and energy to hash out. Think about whether you overreacted or whether the issue hit a personal sensitivity. If you hurt feelings or your feelings became bruised, it may seem more worthwhile to clarify and share forgiveness.

◆ *Value the relationship, not being right.*

How you deal with conflict can be a major positive witness to others around you.

Your primary concern should be caring for and strengthening your relationship with the other person, not winning the argument. Care about the people around you, not about being the most skilled debater.

◆ *Listen first.*

Pretend you are attending a birthday party, and you serve the first piece of cake to the birthday kid. When we let someone else speak first, we show a deep sense of respect and maturity.

Listening better informs us and may straighten out misunderstandings with no other action. It usually makes it easier for others to hear us when it's our turn to talk.

◆ *Focus on objective issues.*

Don't approach conflict based on personal grudges or dislikes. This runs the risk of negatively skewing your vision of the situation. Concern yourself primarily with objective evidence and situations that actually occurred. Focus on what you can do right now to deal with the problem instead of rehashing past situations.

Still, if a situation continues to come up again and again, you may want to try again to get resolution.

◆ *Agree to disagree.*

Sometimes disagreements come to a point where resolution goes nowhere. At that point, for peace and personal health, you may simply need to agree to disagree. If that's the case, move on without holding on to bitterness and resentment.

Ever had a political debate with a close friend who disagrees with your personal opinion, for instance? That's a perfect example of discerning you have different opinions and moving on.

◆ *Forgive others.*

According to a popular phrase, "Unforgiveness is the poison we drink in hoping another will die."

Refusing to forgive others only pollutes our lives and drains us of joy and happiness. Our hope to resolve conflict in a healthy manner fails if we cannot forgive and move on. Do what you can to work through a difficult situation, and then make the choice to forgive and place the matter in God's hands.

◆ *Most of all, don't let conflict tear down your ministry.*

Do everything you can to preserve the well-being of people and your organization. Use conflict to strengthen, not destroy.

It's truly humbling to look back through my life and see how God repaired great tension and hurt in people I loved and worked with for many years.

Several years ago, I found myself bawling in the bathroom over an angry phone call I received from a parent. Unbeknownst to me, this parent was dealing with a lot of stress in her own life, and she manifested her anger in screaming at me over the phone, slinging personal insults that stung my soul.

My assertive personality wanted nothing more than to counterattack, but I instead bit my tongue. I forced myself to listen and try to understand. When she hung up, I rushed to the bathroom and burst into tears, mostly in frustrated rage at enduring her insults without defending myself.

In that situation, I clearly saw God at work. A colleague wisely advised me not to respond until I had my anger completely in check. My irate words could tear down a valuable ministry partner and fledgling youth program.

Eventually, I had a heart-to-heart with this parent, and we worked at rebuilding our relationship. Within a few short years, she became one of my biggest allies, cheering me on and even co-leading a girls' small group with me.

You see, sometimes people drop stress and anger from other situations in "safe" places. People may struggle with financial and marital issues. They may feel helpless as they deal with an alcoholic or drug-addicted family member. Work stress and people problems may overwhelm them. Trapped and frustrated, unable to get help or talk to someone, they often misdirect anger at unknowing innocents, such as utility companies, store clerks, call centers, and church workers.

If you find yourself in a situation where someone's anger seems to outweigh their reported issue, consider if they misplaced their anger. Stay calm. Hear and reflect back their feelings. Avoid defensiveness. Recognize and deal with legitimate gripes. Commiserate in general ways without running down other people or the concerned person. Speak truth in love and let anger diffuse.

Don't waste time burning bridges. Instead, focus on building bridges to share the message of Christ's hope with the world.

Section 2

Recruit, support, and serve with other leaders

I once led a mission trip in the jungle. It was the single worst week I ever experienced.

Nearly faint with crippling heat, constantly swatting mosquitoes and spiders, covered with gritty dirt and melting sunscreen sludge that presumably failed its eight-hour sweat-proof claim, I felt utterly exhausted as I led a hoard of teens through community service.

Fine . . . the truth? It wasn't a jungle, although it felt like it. Actually, it was a mission trip to Florida. Somehow we decided camping at a national park in the middle of summer was a bright idea.

The irony hasn't escaped me, by the way, that I now live in this state I once called a tropical cesspool.

As miserable as the entire trip turned out, one particular day proved the absolute worst. In a mere twenty-four hours, a kid sliced his foot on coral and earned a trip to the emergency room; someone backed a van into a tree and shattered the rear windows; raccoons stole our food and unwittingly caused a food shortage; a giant fight broke out with a group of teenage girls; and every toilet at the campsite unexpectedly clogged, causing a camp-wide emergency.

I watched the leaders around me calmly step in and handle the overwhelming chaos like a skilled team of doctors handling a complicated surgery. In minutes, two precise, detail-oriented leaders whisked our injured student to the hospital. Others quickly patched our broken van with duct tape and cardboard. Two leaders grabbed plungers and solved our bathroom emergency. A thoughtful leader dealt with the female drama, while another focused on singing and goofing around to bring smiles back. Two people quickly adapted a new dinner menu minus the vittles stolen by our furry friends. Everyone else led games and hung out with our students.

Despite so many things going wrong, that day showed me the importance of relying on other capable people. No matter how much I prepared, I never could've handled all of the curve balls thrown in such a short period of time alone. It took an entire team of leaders to make the trip a success.

As I witnessed countless times in my years working with kids and youth, a strong team of leaders makes an incredible impact on your organization. I've been blessed by leaders of all ages serving alongside one another in a variety of different roles. Each brought a special talent no one else could offer to our programs.

Know who volunteers

Percentages of total US population

MEN · WOMEN

21.8% · **27.8%**

Parents with children under 18 years old

36.8 · **45.1**

Most frequent activity

General labor	Food service
12.3	**12.9**
Coach, referee, sports teams	Tutor, teach
9.3	**10.6**
Food service	Fund-raising
9.2	**9.9**

AGES

16–19	26.4
20–24	18.4
25–34	22.3
35–44	28.9
45–54	28.0
55–64	25.1
65+	23.5

Median hours volunteered yearly (all ages)

52

Low	under age 35	
	36 hours	
High	ages 65+	
	94 hours	

Employed	27.2
Part time	31.1
Full time	26.3
Unemployed	23.3
Not in labor force	21.4

Married	29.9
Never married	19.9
Other	20.2

Parents with children under 18	31.3
No children under 18	22.6

Volunteers age 25+

College graduates	38.8
Associate degree, some college	26.5
High school graduates	15.6
No high school diploma	8.1

WHY VOLUNTEERS BECAME INVOLVED

OFFERED	41.6
ASKED	41.2
By boss	1.5
By relative, friend, co-worker	14.5
By organization	23.7
By someone else	1.4
Other	13.4
Not reported	3.8

Organization types

Religious	33.1
Educational, youth service	25.2
Community service, social	14.6

SOURCE: US Bureau of Labor Statistics
www.bls.gov
September 2014 to September 2015

69

Section 2

Without volunteer leaders, I'd flounder alone in a dark, dangerous, and life-sucking whirlpool. However, by partnering together, we reached exponentially more kids and parents, balanced personalities, and supported and uplifted one another.

My fellow leaders constantly challenge, encourage, and inspire me. They complement my strengths and accommodate my weaknesses. They bring a well-rounded energy to our students and families. Because of the diverse people involved in our ministry, we confidently handle nearly every personality and trial that comes our way. Perhaps most critically, working harmoniously shows our entire community how to overcome differences and operate as one united family of believers, serving God together.

I recall studying team ministry in college. We learned how Moses recruited other leaders at the advice of his father-in-law, who said, "You and the people with you will certainly wear yourselves out, for the thing is too heavy for you. You are not able to do it alone" (Exodus 18:18).

Jesus also shared ministry with His disciples. They lived and traveled with Him. They observed and noted His godly decisions, prayer life, and response to needy sinners. Later, He sent teams of disciples to visit villages and prepare them to meet Him. Scripture reports He sent the twelve apostles to heal and proclaim the kingdom of God (Luke 9:1–6). Later, He sent seventy-two disciples to do the same (Luke 10:1–24).

Years later, when I worked in a church, I witnessed firsthand the undeniable impact a team of leaders can have in a ministry and community.

Don't get me wrong, service isn't a walk in the park. It's even more taxing to entrust others to do things related to your passion. Recruiting, training, and working with other leaders can be demanding and difficult. But obvious drawbacks aside, the benefits of shared leadership and its influence on exponentially more people make it well worth the trouble.

Christian leaders show Christ's love to others in everything they do. Yes, this even includes driving a bus full of teens, teaching a Sunday School class, staying up late at a lock-in, leading a small group, or serving alongside students at an event. Together, we participate in Christ's mission to "go therefore and make disciples of all nations" (Matthew 28:19), even in the middle of a hot and humid trip to Florida.

Investing in other leaders is biblical and practical. It broadens your reach to share the Gospel message. Why, then, do so many of us struggle to recruit and work with others?

I suspect, if we answer honestly, much of our hesitation involves our sinfulness. We might worry about being judged inadequate or incapable, or even about losing our position if we let people see how we run things. It may seem like too much work to try to explain tasks to someone else and train them to assist us. We could even feel jealously worried that our students will connect better with someone else.

Perhaps we just hate asking for favors. We think people should volunteer, and we feel annoyed when we have to ask for help. Of course, maybe the truth is that we have no qualms about working in a stagnant ministry.

God didn't bless us with a variety of talents, personalities, and life experiences to squander them wastefully. Our world greatly benefits from the influence of diversity, and our ministries cry out for it.

If you're looking for a way to better your ministry, look no further than to the capable people around you. Kick your sinfulness out of the way.

Recruiting allows others to share in the mission, gives you the opportunity to reach even more individuals, and highlights the blessings of Christ-centered fellowship. As a person actively involved in the mission of reaching students, you can encourage and influence others to join you. So where do you start?

First, identify your needs. Be honest as you assess your strengths and weaknesses candidly without assigning fault or blame. Where does your organization lack support and need improvement?

Perhaps you noticed the same person stuck teaching a group for years, and she needs a partner to encourage her. Maybe you have a lackluster middle school group that needs some fresh faces to liven it up. Perhaps your church hurts for an outreach event, and you need some people to take the bull by the horns and run with it. Write out your needs, and then focus in on the most critical areas for growth.

Even if you're not in charge of a ministry, prayerfully consider ways you can help strengthen the entire organization of a nonprofit, community, or church group.

Prayerfully identify the best possible people to enhance your organization in these areas. Concentrate on finding the best people for your needed roles. Get to know people, strive to understand their personalities, and identify their qualities.

Notice that I didn't say, "Go ahead and grab the nearest human being with a pulse and beg them for help." Come on, what did that poor person getting a cup of coffee ever do to you, anyway?

The awkward part of recruiting is simply asking for help. Acknowledge that you'll feel funny. No one likes to owe a favor, after all. Ask anyway. Take time to share the energy and joy of your organization, and let them know the benefits you think they can bring to the group.

Make every attempt to connect with people one-on-one, and ask to chat in private. I never put individuals on the spot and demand an answer right then and there. I don't guilt them or push them into roles that don't fit. I merely ask people to pray about and consider trying out a new leadership role.

Never fear striking up a conversation with someone about something you feel passionate about. Don't make excuses for someone or think they're too busy or too important to join you. You never know how God might work on their heart or how they might bless others, even if they "just" offer to pray regularly for you and your youth.

Don't feel afraid to try them out for a short season. People often deal with rapidly changing life circumstances, so thoughtfully accommodate them. Suggest a time period or ask them to commit for a time they feel comfortable with, such as three months, six months, or a year.

If someone says no, ask again later. Even if it's not the perfect time for them to get involved, you may plant a seed of interest and they'll seek you out in the future. Remember that you're not asking for you, but for the sake of the eternal lives of the children entrusted to you.

Often, people hesitate to volunteer because they worry that if they say yes, it means signing up for a lifetime of slaving away in this role. I once took over a Sunday School program and had ten leaders quit simultaneously. I quickly discovered that all ten leaders jumped ship because they had felt guilted into staying for nearly a decade, despite numerous pleas for help. As a fresh face, I didn't guilt them into serving for the rest of their lives.

When working with others, make sure to provide a clear understanding of expectations. Every organization benefits from members who understand the roles they fulfill and the clear standards for them as leaders.

Ideally, great people united as one team will strengthen your group and help handle the ebbs of ministry. Encourage each leader to look for other great leaders you can bring into your group and train as well.

Working with students means that leaders fill many roles—cheerleader, listening ear, counselor, shoulder to cry on, friend, mentor, disciplinarian, voice of experience, and occasionally goofball.

God calls us in all of these roles to love these kids the way that Christ loves them and to help them grow in their faith in their heavenly Father.

I boil down my expectations for leaders into a few simple points.

- ◆ **Christ is number one in everything.**

    Our whole life as Christians, and everything we are about as leaders, centers in Christ.

    We belong to God because He sent His only Son as our Savior. Because of Jesus' death and resurrection, our sins are forgiven and we have a new life. We receive His gifts through God's Word, Baptism, and the Lord's Supper. Through these, the Holy Spirit works faith in us. This faith gives us a unique voice in a world of confusion and chaos.

    In the same ways, God also gave these gifts to the students we serve. Nothing is more important than continuing to share that beautiful faith in everything we do!

The rest of the leader expectations help us work together as we live and serve in this one true faith.

◆ *Be a prayer warrior.*

Every day, leaders potentially face incredibly complex decisions and difficult emotions from students. I encourage you and those you work with to observe what Abraham Lincoln once said: "I have been driven many times to my knees by the overwhelming conviction that I had nowhere else to go."

◆ *Be a Christlike example.*

We all know the old phrase "Actions speak louder than words."

Students watch adults closely and pick up more than they ever let us know. I encourage leaders to immerse themselves in regular church attendance, Bible studies, and other church and community activities. I also encourage them to show Christ in their attitudes toward church leaders and one another.

Kids can spot gossip, jealousy, and discontent, however carefully hidden, a mile away. An effective team strives to show Christ's love to one another and to others.

◆ *Hang out with your kids.*

This sounds like a no-brainer, but I often spot leaders talking to one another and spending more time together than they do with students. Our ministry is not about spending quality time with fellow adults; it's about the kids.

Sometimes leaders become focused on cell phones or social media and ignore the people in front of them.

We may offer the only opportunity some kids have to spend quality time with caring Christian adults. Leaders need to make the most of the time and save tasks for another time. I tell my leaders, "You may be the only Bible that someone ever reads."

◆ *Keep control of your kids.*

Always remember that students will walk all over you if you let them. I encourage leaders to keep a healthy rein on their kids. I let them know it's perfectly acceptable to have students clean up their own messes, throw away their trash, push their chairs in, hold open doors, and respect property.

Adults also keep control of discussion topics and make sure students share appropriately.

◆ *Keep me in the loop.*

Since I manage many kids at a time, I don't need to know about every single situation that arises. If a serious problem comes up or adults get stuck in a situation they don't feel confident dealing with, I encourage them to loop me in right away. I can't help them if I'm totally clueless.

I also encourage leaders to update me regularly and as needed. I ask them to share major changes in students' behavior, family situations, friendships, appearance, or attitude confidentially between ministry leaders. Many eyes need to watch and help a struggling child.

◆ *Be prepared.*

Good leaders always prepare, and the best leaders prepare for everything to go wrong. I often remind our leaders to plan their lessons, activities, and events carefully. I ask them to have a plan, a backup plan, and a backup-backup plan.

It's a good idea to bring things to keep kids busy during downtime, such as a deck of cards, a trivia book, or a fun activity in your back hip pocket. It's helpful to always have a few go-to games ready to pull out at a moment's notice.

Clear expectations like these greatly benefit every team of leaders. They provide an understanding of how to work with one another and the kids and families we serve. Ministry jobs can often seem overwhelming, but we need to cut to the heart of what we expect from leaders.

And when we care for those little sheep well, we can have a little peace too.

I've been privileged to see Romans 15:5–6 lived out by my leaders: "May the God of endurance and encouragement grant you to live in such harmony with one another, in accord with Christ Jesus, that together you may with one voice glorify the God and Father of our Lord Jesus Christ."

Service as a leader involves many important tasks. It's crucial to corral your mind-set and focus on patiently loving those around you. Your humble attitude matters as you seek to serve children and teens. You must understand how to support families and co-workers. You need to carefully prepare safety plans and practices.

The role of youth workers delicately mixes self-awareness and humility, seasons with a dash of enthusiasm and fun, and tempers with wisdom, patience, and encouragement. We are truth-givers, the champions of sharing faith, love, and acceptance.

Above all, we have been charged with the responsibility of improving the well-being of other humans, often when they aren't always capable of making the best decisions for themselves.

Even if you feel apprehensive about serving, move ahead confidently with knowledge that God placed you right where He wants you. As you work faithfully with the students God placed around you, share your inimitable talents and one-of-a-kind personality to inspire, lead, teach, and uplift others.

As the Holy Spirit works in and through us, we live out His incredible story of mercy, grace, and peace in Christ Jesus.

Section 3:
Working with kids & youth

Untrue stereotypes of today's youth

*When I was in junior high, my Sunday School
class struck fear in the hearts of adults.*

We were quite proud that our class held the record for teacher turnover in the entire church, averaging a new teacher about every two weeks. Our Sunday School superintendent couldn't find a single adult who actually wanted to teach our class. Often, we sat in the classroom alone on Sunday morning, wreaking havoc on the craft closet when yet another teacher admitted defeat and failed to show up.

I shudder to think of the pranks we played while unsupervised. Let's just say that we managed to unravel an entire closet full of yarn in mere minutes, and we had quite a flair for hanging it from ceiling fans.

As troublesome as my little junior high class was, we weren't really bad kids. A smart group, ravenous for deeper knowledge, we hungered for adults who would actually stand up to us and not give in to our teasing demands. However, our reputation as a difficult class grew until no adult in our congregation wanted anything to do with us. Even as a twelve-year-old, the label as a rabble-rousing class bothered me.

When I look back on my own childhood, I see many other inaccurate stereotypes teachers and leaders projected onto my peers and me. These hurtful labels inflamed sensitive young minds and caused kids to feel alone and misunderstood.

Ministry to kids and teens is rife with misconceptions. While some judgments are well founded, others miss the mark.

If we desire to impact kids, we must acknowledge their true selves and not give in to common characterizations society tacks onto their generation. Of course, we can generalize based on biology, statistics, knowledge, and firsthand experience, but many stereotypes ring as untrue.

Here are some of the popular stereotypes about the younger generation and the truth behind them.

Stereotype 1: Kids can't focus.

The truth? They can, but you must understand *how* they focus.

When I first started in youth ministry, I felt like a glorified babysitter, prepared with decks of cards and oodles of games in order to keep my wild kids amused long enough to survive the hour.

I unfairly discounted the interest my young students had in what I taught. Gradually, I realized that children actually have a deep desire to learn. Though kids have varying learning styles and levels of comprehension, they also are curious about the world around them, excited about life, and full of questions.

By abandoning the untrue thought that kids can't focus and tailoring our lessons to their unique age level, we can impact them greatly. Students can realistically focus for the entire length of a lesson, provided you show them how the lesson applies to their lives and engage them through a variety of tactics that address their different learning styles. Use movie and music clips, activities, experiences, and games.

When we give full attention and speak from the heart, kids respond in kind.

Stereotype 2: You can't tear students away from technology.

The truth? Kids long for time to unplug.

For years, I've taken kids on mission trips and retreats sans cell phones and electronic gadgets. Ironically, kids never get upset about leaving their technology at home. Parents raise issues, insisting their kids can't handle separation from their gadgets.

This generation of students is more technologically savvy and connected than any other in world history. But they admit they want time away from this fast-paced, draining world. In the last few years, scores of kids admitted they would love to go off and live simply in the wilderness, without worrying about maintaining social media profiles, responding to texts, or looking things up online.

Don't fear separating kids from technology for some good old-fashioned face-to-face time. By offering our kids a regular chance to unplug and unwind, even by simply turning off their phones for the hour in class or youth group, we give them a chance to fully concentrate on being human again.

The first time you ask students to unplug, they may object. In a short time, they see the value and resist arguing. They even remind one another to put away their devices and join the group.

Stereotype 3: Today's kids are spoiled and care only about themselves.

The truth? This generation cares deeply about the world.

Though studies cite children today as some of the most entitled individuals in history, they also connect globally more than any other generation.

Their daily routine of surfing the Internet exposes them to a bevy of issues all around the world, from poverty and hunger to self-harm, genocide, and terrorism. Today's youngsters have a strong desire to fix the world in their own unique way. They may combat a problem by making a creative video, starting a social media campaign, or serving with a nonprofit organization.

Section 3

Though most kids are self-focused, a normal trait for typical developing adolescents, they also exhibit keen interest in social justice and global relations. Harness this passion by providing plenty of opportunities for dialogue about problems in the world and what individuals and groups can do to address and overcome these troubles.

Stereotype 4: Students relate only to a young leader.

The truth? Today's children look up to a variety of individuals.

Quick, describe what a youth leader looks like to you. Did you picture a twenty-something individual with perfectly mussed hair in jeans, trendy shoes, and an ironic T-shirt?

Somehow, our culture created the inaccurate stereotype that kids, particularly teens, relate only to a cool, good-looking young leader. We hopelessly resigned everyone over the age of thirty as fairly irrelevant to the lives of our children. And while our students definitely connect with and look up to younger leaders, they also relate to people of all ages.

I personally witnessed grandparents, aunts, uncles, older adults, college students, and high schoolers all make incredible connections with kids of all ages. Even though you may not fit into a societal expectation of what a youth leader looks like, the Holy Spirit can use your unique personality, talents, and traits to reach others. So don't write off anyone as a possible and invaluable leader for kids.

Stereotype 5: Students care only about playing games.

The truth? Kids want authenticity and depth.

Watching kids on a playground shows that children love laughing, running around together, and playing games. However, our ministry needs to go far beyond stringing together an endless array of games and activities.

In ministering to students, we have the opportunity to stand beside kids when they first face some of the most challenging situations of their lives. It's our privilege to share what a relationship with Christ is like and to connect with students before the world irreversibly jades them.

Don't cheat your students by giving them junk food when what they really desire is the Bread of Life. Give them chances to be real and dive headfirst into the truth about serious life issues like relationships, intimacy, brokenness, sin, forgiveness, and grace.

Stereotype 6: Student ministry has a one-size-fits-all solution.

The truth? Each ministry has its own unique personality.

Students of all ages struggle with similar issues, such as identity, image, self-discipline, change, questions about the future, and relationship difficulties. However, each community owns a unique identity, and every student in that community deals with different issues.

For example, I used to work with many kids who dealt with promiscuity and severe alcohol and drug abuse in their public middle school. The kids I currently teach in a private school deal mainly with relationship drama and frustration with parental expectations. Different communities and cultures bring different challenges to the children within them.

No single magic solution works for every ministry in every city in the world. Rather than focus on finding the perfect curriculum, book, or program, concentrate on understanding your particular context and tweaking resources to fit the needs of your students. God placed you in this place, so ask for His wisdom as you teach His children.

Stereotype 7: Kids are too difficult to teach.

The truth? Children soak up the love we give them.

Adjectives adults often use to paint a picture of kids could also describe wild beasts. Though I'd certainly admit some animal-like tendencies in some youth, especially when it comes to feeding them in public, they're not the insane creatures some people perceive.

Frankly, the accusation that children are too difficult to teach usually comes from people who don't understand how to work with kids or who fail to adequately prepare their lesson or supplies for their time together.

In my life, students emerged as my biggest encouragers and the most thoughtful, caring individuals I ever encountered. Whether they doodle a picture for me after a long day, leave a note of appreciation on my desk, or text me a funny joke, they constantly share love with me.

My middle school religion classes prayed for me nearly daily as I wrote this book. They endlessly supported me. For the most part, kids demonstrate understanding, patience, and caring. They adore the diverse collection of leaders in their lives and have more than enough love to share with everyone.

Section 3

Stereotype 8: Ministry to kids isn't as important as other ministries.

The truth? It's of critical importance.

People who chronically underfund, discount, and write off the importance of working with kids perpetuate this stereotype.

Jesus thought otherwise. He welcomed children, prostitutes, tax collectors, and other societal outcasts. Those who misunderstood opposed Him and gave Him quite an earful.

Quite simply, research shows that potential for lifelong faith impact is greater in childhood than at any other age. The Barna Research Group found that most people respond to the value of Jesus Christ's life, death, and resurrection before the age of eighteen. In fact, a majority of Americans do so by age 12. (*Research Shows That Spiritual Maturity Process Should Start at a Young Age*, © The Barna Group Ltd., published online at www.barna.org on November 17, 2003.)

We simply cannot discount the importance of Christian leaders working with children and adolescents. In this swirling storm of questioning, doubting, venturing into a world full of temptation, and stepping out in faith, we serve as a beacon of hope. We have the chance to capture kids as their spiritual development buds. What an opportune time for the Holy Spirit to capture the hearts of students as they form personal identities and beliefs.

We have the chance to influence the future by working with children. In the famous words of Frederick Douglass, "It is easier to build strong children than to repair broken men."

Stereotype 9: You need to have all the answers.

The truth? It's not really about you. It's about Jesus.

So often, leaders bemoan their own lack of knowledge, confiding, "I don't know the Bible that well, so how can I possibly teach kids about God?" Other times, great leaders let their pasts get in the way, detailing their wild years and thinking kids would never respect them if they knew their stories.

Here's the truth: this work isn't about you. It doesn't really matter if you flawlessly hold the attention of a group, if kids laugh at your hilarious jokes and pranks, or if you present creative and unique lessons. It doesn't matter if you're the "cool leader," wear the right clothes, and use the most current slang. It doesn't matter if you published a slew of books, take on many speaking gigs, or clock more years working with kids than anyone else.

The work we do is all about Christ: who He is and what He did for us by dying on the cross and rising from the dead. He saved us from our sins and gave us eternal life with Him. We help students discover this profound, life-altering truth about Jesus as we share God's Word with them. We teach kids how to develop and sustain a relationship with Christ. We share the message of love with those who don't yet know Jesus as their Savior.

That false stereotype that tempts you to think ministry is all about you? It's not from God. Don't focus on thinking you aren't good enough or don't have adequate knowledge. Instead, lower yourself to your knees and give your attention to your heavenly Father. He promises to fortify you with the wisdom and strength you need to serve the kids.

In fact, the Lord specializes in using weak, sinful people to do His work. Through St. Paul, the Lord revealed, "God chose what is foolish in the world to shame the wise; God chose what is weak in the world to shame the strong; God chose what is low and despised in the world, even things that are not, to bring to nothing things that are, so that no human being might boast in the presence of God. And because of Him you are in Christ Jesus, who became to us wisdom from God, righteousness and sanctification and redemption" (1 Corinthians 1:27–30).

And God promised, "Likewise the Spirit helps us in our weakness. For we do not know what to pray for as we ought, but the Spirit Himself intercedes for us with groanings too deep for words" (Romans 8:26).

The longer I do ministry, the more I realize how little I know and how I must rely on the Holy Spirit to intercede in my thoughts and actions to capture moments for Christ. Only through the wisdom and knowledge impressed on my heart by the Holy Spirit through God's Word and the guidance of other mature Christians can I sort out His truth from falsehoods, stereotypes, and other worldly wisdom.

Together, we can dispel these untrue stereotypes and junk our inaccurate judgments. We can see our students as eager to learn, grow, and change the world. Our youth aren't future leaders; they're leaders now. So let's do our best to raise them up, treat them with respect, and give them the credit they justly deserve.

Crafting relevant learning experiences

The janitors hated me, and they told me so to my face.

In a previous youth ministry position, I earned a reputation of doing the oddest, most bizarre, and often smelliest and messiest object lessons known to mankind. Though I always cleaned up, our poor janitors often found themselves taking out buckets of disgusting trash and digging sprinkles out of crevices in the floor.

One time in particular, we all learned the hard way not to play Messy Twister with chocolate sauce and mustard and leave it in the garbage can overnight.

Though I was the bane of my janitors' existence, we drew many kids deeply into Scripture through our unusual lessons. Through creative and zany activities, we hooked youth into faith discovery and kept their attention.

As leaders, we stand on the front lines of crafting relevant learning experiences for our youth. Whether we have them for twenty minutes in a classroom, or for a week on a mission trip, we filter and screen lessons, tailoring them to our students' lives.

It's our duty to know our students, their struggles, and their personalities well so that we can come alongside them and provide them with thought-provoking material that fans the flames of their faith. Think of it as the difference between blindly shooting at a target in the dark and hoping to hit the target versus aiming intentionally with a well-placed bullet.

In working with kids of all ages, I promise that it's much more effective to spend a bit of time preparing rather than just grabbing a lesson off a shelf and expecting it to engage your students.

Leaders often ask me how exactly to tailor materials to their students.

First, know your kids and your community. Analyze their culture. Find out about their family life and interests. Know what affects them and what their friends talk about in the hall at school. Discover what they look at online. Discern what keeps them up at night with worry. Pay attention to what excites them.

Knowing these things tells you what part of God's Word will capture them best. It lets you speak the most applicable truth confidently to them.

Second, take time to prepare intentionally impactful lessons. Different educators teach various models for creating lessons, but I use an easy rule of thumb I learned in college: Hook, Book, Look, and Took. (Hook, Book, Look, Took model described in *Creative Bible Teaching* by Larry O. Richards, © 1970 by Moody Bible Institute of Chicago. Revised and expanded in 1998 with Gary J. Bredfeldt.)

Whether you write a lesson from scratch or enhance a resource, this model provides a helpful structure.

Start lessons with a Hook, an activity, question, or experience that grabs attention or hooks your kids. A Hook doesn't necessarily need to be biblical, but it should create a sense of excitement. Avoid yes-or-no questions; choose something that sparks interest. Ideas for a Hook include thought-provoking video clips, music, odd objects, and unexpected questions. One easy Hook I used plenty of times involves a Minute to Win It–style game that relates to the topic of the day.

What does this look like, practically? Let me give you an example. Let's say I plan to talk about selfishness. I could hold up a ten dollar bill and have students compete in a paper, rock, scissors tournament to see who wins the money. That could easily lead into a discussion on how our culture chases wealth and where that desire stems from, our sinful and selfish nature.

One important thing to know about today's kids is, perhaps more than any other generation, they need to know why they should pay attention. If we can answer their query of why our message matters, we raise our chances of securely gripping their attention.

After your Hook, move on to the Book. This step helps students discover biblical truths and make scriptural observations. In other words, you dig into your Bible.

Typically, Book activities relate to your lesson opening. They guide the discussion into what people need to know: the who, what, where, when, and how. Use questions such as "According to these verses, what gives happiness?" and "Where was Jesus when He said this to the disciples?"

As you lead students into Scripture, take care to use a variety of different methods because individuals easily tire of repeating the same thing. For example, to move beyond discussion questions, ask students to sum up a Bible chapter with a 140-character Twitter message or create a skit about a parable.

Next, move into the Look section of your lesson, where students summarize, reflect on, and respond to what they learned from the Book section. Look reinforces key discoveries and truths you discussed and prompts participants to make life applications. In a nutshell, this is where we look at how the Bible applies directly to us. Possible questions might include "What can we learn from the early believers about the importance of community?" and "What difference does a Christ-centered community make in your daily life?"

The last part of this model uses Took. This represents your intentional effort to give your students something to take home with them so they can live out what they learned. That doesn't mean sending them home with a work sheet. It means sending students out the door with a mind-melting question or challenge to think about long after they leave the room.

Section 3

The end of your lesson presents an opportunity to make the lesson personal. Let students speak about specific applications of the truth they discovered together. Get personal, specific, and detailed. For example, ask, "What will you do next time you feel afraid?" or "What did you learn about trusting the Lord?" Let them share a favorite Bible verse from the lesson or identify a phrase to say to themselves each day of the next week.

Be careful not to end with a works-oriented focus, advising your students that they need to "be better." This message often sneaks into kids' lessons. Teachers often kick tykes out the door with "Don't hit your sister this week!" instead of a message about forgiveness and grace when you do hit your sister.

Learning styles and how they impact those you lead

Sometimes you simply need to think like a toddler.

No, don't throw a temper tantrum because you really, really want ice cream for breakfast.

Think like a toddler. What do I mean? When you watch these tiny tots, you see high-energy little kids running around nonstop, listening, moving, looking, and playing. Just as a toddler craves a rich variety of experiences, people of all ages learn best when we use different activities, experiences, and discussions.

Engage multiple learning styles to offer variety in learning experiences. Every person has a primary learning style and one or more secondary styles. However, everyone benefits from doing different activities. We even benefit from using our least likely style.

Most people tend to teach how they prefer to learn. To reach everyone, we must intentionally teach with strategies that engage a variety of learning styles. This creates an environment where everyone can learn, not just those who learn as we do. Use these principles to plan lessons that powerfully impact students.

Generally, educators identify seven general categories of learning styles.

◆ *Visual learners*

Visual learners learn best by looking at pictures, colors, and charts. They often use colors and layout to organize their thoughts, such as using different colors of folders for different subjects or high-lighting test notes with different colors. They respond well to object lessons and movie clips.

Visual learners also love to see information. They prefer looking at notes on the board and taking notes themselves. They tend to watch their teachers' body language closely. In other words, they notice when you feel bored, confused, or excited about a lesson. They often like a clean and uncluttered place to learn and study.

◆ *Auditory learners*

Auditory learners prefer to listen to sounds, rhyme, music, and speech. They learn well from listening to recordings and jingles. They love to memorize information by putting words to music or

Learning Styles

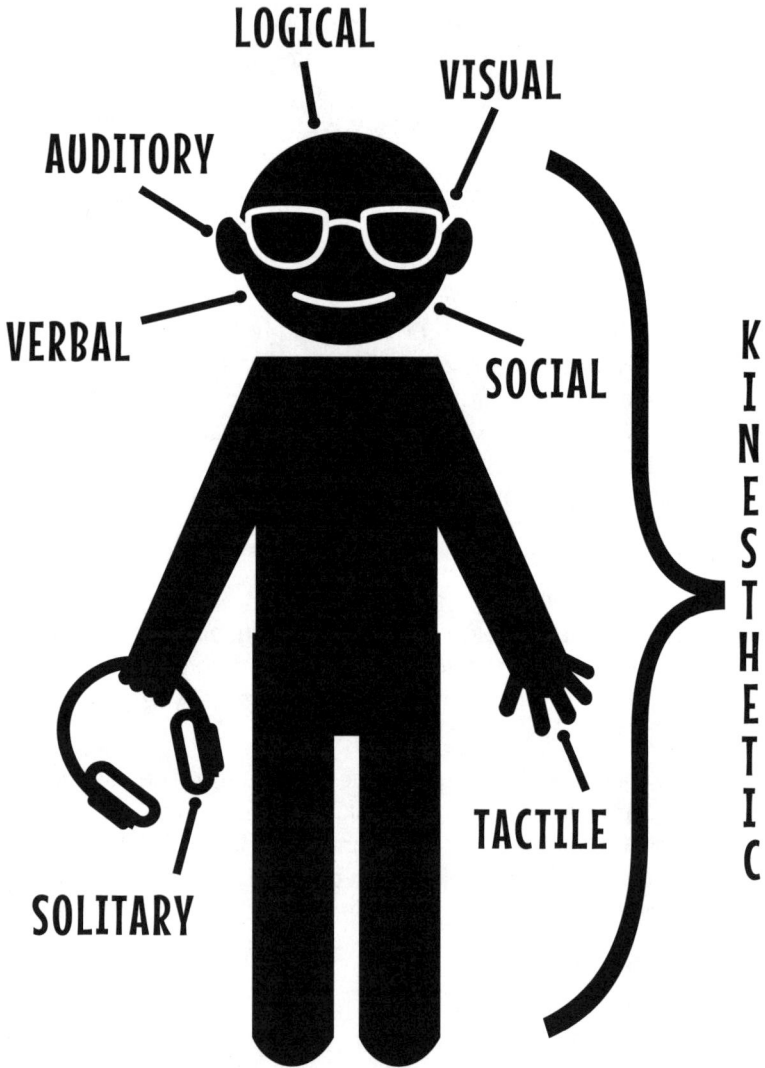

LOGICAL

VISUAL

AUDITORY

VERBAL

SOCIAL

KINESTHETIC

TACTILE

SOLITARY

Art © Shutterstock, Inc.

by making up mnemonic ditties. They enjoy listening to a song or speech and talking about its meaning.

Auditory learners learn best by hearing and discussing information. They tend to ask many questions, wholeheartedly dive into debates, and get the group chatting about a subject. Typically, they don't like to take notes or read; they lose interest during these tasks. This type responds well to music. They often clamor to listen to the radio or music while working.

◆ *Verbal learners*

Verbal learners benefit from word usage in speech and writing. They enjoy reading and listening to lectures or sermons and extracting information from these sources.

An individual best captures their attention through varying voice inflections. They like reading aloud or listening to someone read a story dramatically.

◆ *Physical learners*

Kinesthetic learners like to use their whole bodies to learn. They enjoy getting out of their seat and doing something. Activities include touching or feeling something, playing a game, molding something, drawing a diagram, and role-playing.

Kinesthetic learners also love hands-on, multisensory experiences. Their interest sparks most when they have the opportunity to do things as they learn new concepts, such as learning about castles while building one out of blocks.

Teachers engage them best through "living lessons" where they can manipulate materials and move their bodies. They prefer not to sit and listen to someone.

Similarly, tactile learners learn best when they can touch or fiddle with things. Interestingly, these types of learners tend to doodle while they listen, as a way of keeping themselves engaged.

◆ *Logical learners*

Logical learners enjoy reasoning, analyzing, and facts. They tend to understand systems and organization easily. They often create and use lists to organize their thoughts.

They enjoy hearing the context of stories or activities because they like to understand the whole picture. Logical minds benefit from hearing the background setting of a Bible story and appreciate independent confirmation of information. They love bullet points.

◆ *Social learners*

Social learners love to connect with others in learning, whether a partner, small group, or larger group. They learn best when they discover something and share it with others.

Often extroverted, these socially minded learners love tackling the dynamics of a group to process information. They enjoy talking through a subject together. They love participating in debates, dramas, and role-plays in groups.

◆ *Solitary learners*

Solitary learners do their best thinking by themselves. They like to work and study alone. Often, they find a deep personal interest in a topic and work independently to learn more about it in private.

They enjoy solitary writing or reflection time, such as breaking away from the group for a few minutes of silent prayer or to respond to a closing question.

Practical tips for teaching kids and youth

*Washing my hair for the fourth time to no avail, I
realized my head resembled a Halloween wig.*

It started innocently. One of my students creatively suggested a flour war for a youth event. We took tiny handfuls of flour packed in tissues and tossed them at one another in the parking lot, like little grenades. An hour later, when everyone was thoroughly covered in white flour from head to toe, a freak rain shower passed over.

Though I was able to clean my clothes, my hair was another story. I had been hit in the head so many times with flour bombs that my blond hair turned vivid white. The rain hardened the immense amount of flour to a cement-like consistency.

It took days to get all the flour out of my hair.

Sometimes we learn lessons only through experiences. In this case, a miserable experience taught me not to play with flour on days with precipitation in the forecast.

Experience is the wisest teacher when it comes to teaching kids too. As Johann Goethe once said, "By seeking and blundering we learn."

It can sometimes seem daunting to put everything you learned and read into practice, but don't feel afraid to try. Every good leader has to start somewhere, and you'll likely learn best from mistakes you make. Fortunately, kids are resilient and hungry to learn. They tend to bounce back easily, even when you think a lesson fell flat.

In my many years of trial and error, I picked up a number of simple, practical tips for teaching kids and youth.

◆ ***Draw inspiration from a muse.***

In art, a muse is the source of inspiration for an artist. Though it seems a little odd, find your own muse in your group and let that person inspire how you fashion lessons.

My muse of many years was a kid named Josh—bright, goofy, and always running around, playing with everything in sight. I carefully considered Josh every time I planned an event. Whether retreat or small-group study, if I thought an activity could grip and keep his attention, I went for it.

Having a specific person in mind as a target for learning experiences became vastly helpful.

◆ *Plan elements for all learning styles.*

Make sure you intentionally include a wide variety of activities within each lesson you teach. This is a surefire way to keep people interested in your topic. Include elements such as movie clips, games, songs, debates, object lessons, art projects, movement, singing, discussion, hands-on activities, solo thinking time, and prayer.

By hitting on multiple learning styles in creative ways, you keep the attention of the entire group.

◆ *Know your lesson well.*

One of the biggest rookie mistakes I see people make is not knowing their lessons well enough to actually engage with kids. Stuck reading their notes, leaders quickly lose kids' attention. Make sure you adequately prepare for teaching. Read through your materials a few times to get a solid idea of order and content.

Remember, a lesson is merely a guide, not a script. I recommend memorizing your first few points to ease you into the flow of leading. Make sure you always look ahead to know your next question, point, or activity before you get to it. Some leaders write brief outlines or list short phrases to remind themselves what to do next.

The last thing you want to do is pause to find your place again. Thirty seconds of dead time will cost you several minutes in refocusing the group.

◆ *Carefully consider room arrangement.*

Never underestimate the power of how people function in a setting! Plan your room carefully. Do you need space for games? Do you want kids to sit and take notes from the board? Do you want people to open up and enjoy stimulating dialogue with one another?

To encourage discussion for kids of any age, the most practical tip I can offer is to ditch the formal desks. Instead, gather people on the floor in a circle. This simple act with more casual posture lowers inhibitions. Eye-to-eye interaction makes a big difference in helping people open up to one another. If your group can't handle the freedom of sitting on the floor, try sitting in a circle of chairs.

◆ *Use simple, repetitive language and themes.*

Use simple, repeating language and themes throughout your lessons to best make your point. This becomes especially important when you work with young children. They love to learn through repetitive songs, games, phrases, and rhymes.

Pick a central theme and expand it with no more than a few key teaching points.

◆ *Accept the "fleeting aha!"*

Don't give in to the temptation of thinking you always get to see lessons connect powerfully with students. Sometimes all you get is a slight pause, an agape mouth, a change in body language, or a flash of interest in someone's eyes. I call this the "fleeting aha." Although a lesson or spiritual truth makes a big impact on someone, that moment in which you tangibly see the impact made never lasts long, as kids quickly rebound from emotional moments. Just because teens don't spend hours quietly contemplating your lesson doesn't discount the profound effect that the lesson may have in their lives.

To inspire learning and impart wisdom is an incredible opportunity. The words of Cornelius Plantiga couldn't ring any truer in my own experiences: "We know the excitement of getting a present—we love to unwrap it to see what is inside. So it is with our children. They are gifts we unwrap for years as we discover the unique characters God has made them."

Handling discipline

A student almost ran me over with my own car.

Yes, it's true. And if you're keeping track, I work with a lot of younger kids. Which makes it all that much worse when I say I was hijacked and my keys were stolen from me.

I sprinted to my car just in time to see one of my fourteen-year-old boys trying to back out of the parking space. I blocked him by standing squarely behind the vehicle.

Suffice it to say that no one got hurt, nor did my vehicle get damaged in any way.

In fact, the expression on my face alone terrified this troublesome student so much that he immediately hopped out of my seat, meekly climbed into the back of the car, and remained silent the entire ride back. He wrote me an extensive letter of apology on Facebook that very night. We had a long and stern talk about his behavior and set guidelines for future behavior in and around my car.

Despite the fact that I was very angry with him and let him know it, our relationship today is better than ever.

Discipline. Anyone who works with children or teens encounters and deals with its alternately maddening and satisfying twists and turns. I worked with dozens of great leaders over the last few years, and a lot of them really struggled with the issue of discipline. In fact, I'd venture a guess that most people consider discipline a tricky subject.

Here are several common myths I encountered regarding discipline.

Myth 1: Discipline happens only to address misbehavior.

People often view discipline as a treatment for bad behavior eruptions.

In reality, discipline should become part of the fabric of our entire ministry. It should reflect the pride and standards we set for our youth and ourselves. And properly placed discipline produces far fewer crisis situations.

Myth 2: Discipline is optional.

At some point, we all experience situations that require loving but firm doses of discipline. Turning the other cheek to bad behavior does nothing but store problems for the future.

We can't just walk through life thinking that problems will never arise. We need to develop a cohesive discipline plan beforehand.

Myth 3: Discipline gives you an excuse for your temper.

No, discipline is not an excuse to blow your top.

In fact, the angrier you feel, the less likely you'll discipline your students properly.

Remember the old adage "Count to ten before you react"? In youth ministry, sometimes it's wise to count to fifty. Walk away, disengage, and do whatever it takes to calm yourself down so you don't discipline someone in the heat of the moment. Just don't leave them alone with glow sticks!

Myth 4: Discipline means you hate someone.

We don't discipline out of dislike but out of love.

The act of disciplining shows our students we care so much about them that we're willing to do something that might make us feel uncomfortable. Yes, this means even risking a precious relationship to help them grow into mature, responsible adults. That's a powerful statement, no matter how squirrelly the kid.

Myth 5: Discipline ruins relationships.

Sometimes we fear acting on our own rules and laying down the law because we don't want to ruin our relationship with a student. We've all been there, thinking, "If I tell him to cut it out, maybe he won't ever come back!"

If you lay out ground rules properly and discipline appropriately and sensitively, your relationship with that particular youth can become even stronger than ever.

Throughout my years of disciplining students, I most often end up closer to students because we shared experiences of working through rough times, even when I punished them. Students typically realize it takes more love to speak honestly and work together to change bad behavior. They respect that effort.

Despite the many frustrating experiences some troublemakers put me through, showing them that I'm there for them in the long haul enhanced our relationships.

Myth 6: Discipline is a perfect craft.

You'll make mistakes. Lots of them.

This is one of the most important things I learned about working with kids.

Sometimes, mistakes involve overreacting and snapping at kids. I once had a very sweet and sensitive young lady wrong me when I felt stressed out while leading a mission trip. She apologized to me, and I snapped back, "You better just pray that God changes my heart, because I'm sure not ready to talk to you right now!" Ouch.

Apologize, admit your mistakes, and move on.

That's the amazing thing about working with youth. They'd rather have honesty than perfection from their leaders. As Tim, one of my middle school students, told me, "I know sometimes adults discipline me just because they're scared and don't know what to do."

You're human. Don't worry, your students get that.

Truths that inform discipline

So now the question remains, how do you build discipline into your ministry?

Truth 1: Act proactively.

Don't wait for problems to emerge before addressing them.

Instead, talk about rules, relationships you want to build, and possible areas of temptation to try to cut off trouble before it arrives. Put yourself in the shoes of your most mischievous student. What could he or she possibly do? Thinking like that while planning events helps identify a whole slew of issues that could arise and helps you plan discipline accordingly.

You don't need to spend a lot of time dwelling on the ideas of punishment, rewards, or penalties. Simply set up expectations right away, and have a plan ready for when issues arise. Remember, always enforce consequences fairly and consistently.

Truth 2: Limit explanations.

Don't spend time listening to long explanations.

Explanations of bad behavior are usually flimsy excuses. Your students will use explanations to shift blame elsewhere, which only distracts and demoralizes you. Focus on how you can actually better the situation, instead of spending time listening to your kids perfect their creative storytelling.

However, don't completely gloss over what kids say. Give students a limited window to clarify something you may not understand. Get the facts so you fully understand the situation before making a judgment and taking action.

As sixth grader Roxy said, "Adults don't always take the time to understand what's going on. They discipline automatically, without thinking or pausing. Sometimes they jump to conclusions. They discipline you for doing something they assume you do, and they lose trust in you, all because they didn't take the time to understand what actually happened."

Truth 3: Promote ownership.

The more teens invest in the group, the more they police themselves.

"Hey, Lucy, stop that! You're ruining it for the rest of us!"

A good youth ministry aims to build a sense of pride and identity within its members, as well as an open attitude toward new people.

The dynamics of your group should encourage kids to develop their own sense of self-discipline and ownership. Give opportunities for students to participate in leadership, such as delegating a certain student to get your group seated and ready to learn or letting a class rate themselves on their behavior in the middle of class.

Truth 4: Be calm and logical.

It's easy to feel frazzled and want to react to a troublesome student in anger.

In this moment, though, you have the ability to demonstrate love and self-control in a powerful way, something a student obviously needs in her life. Never lose your temper and blow up at a student. Approach an issue logically, like a police officer might objectively approach a sensitive situation, not emotionally.

As middle schooler Julia advises, "Don't use a harsh voice. Be calm when you discipline us, so I can understand you."

Adam, another student, agrees. "Hear me out without cutting me off or interrupting me or shouting. Shouting makes me want to shout back, which causes you to shout back, which creates a vicious cycle. Be calm and collected, and let me really talk to you about the situation."

Truth 5: Work together.

If you have a team of leaders or volunteers, make sure to work together. Share approaches, support one another, pool information about teens who need more help and guidance than others, and back one another up.

Make it impossible for kids to play one leader against another by using effective communication systems carefully set in place in advance. I learned the hard way that even the most trustworthy teens will attempt to sabotage leaders' words to get what they want. Be prepared by always staying on the same page with your leadership team.

Truth 6: Get on your knees in prayer.

Never underestimate taking time to call on the Lord!

Immerse yourself in God's Word on a regular basis, and pray regularly for discernment and wisdom as a youth leader. It's not an easy job to do, but God Himself equipped and called you to this vocation. As a wise friend once told me, "God doesn't call the qualified; He qualifies the called."

Discipline strategies

What do you do when you actually need to discipline students? Here are some helpful hints.

Strategy 1: Pull students aside individually.

Never, ever attempt to correct a student in front of the whole group unless she's doing something life-threatening. Remember, no matter how much bravado you think your students have, childhood is still a time of fragile self-esteem for most students. So pull your problem child aside in private and begin a conversation.

Make sure someone else handles the group while you deal with this individual in another location. Or wait until class finishes to approach your student.

As seventh grader Will advised me, "Don't ever humiliate kids in front of others. That humiliation always sticks with you. It becomes a horrible memory in your mind."

Strategy 2: Be clear about infractions.

Address issues directly.

If someone caused a problem with the entire group, help your student see how his actions distracted others. Usually a student knows this, but sometimes the kid is so self-absorbed that he doesn't realize how he affected those around him. Point it out gently. Use humor to your advantage to soften the blow of a harsh rebuke while still making your meaning clear.

Strategy 3: Show grace.

Be strong and firm, but quickly follow up with grace and love.

Use firm statements to express your true feelings, such as "I never want to see you do that again because it's not appropriate" (and everyone in this room needs two eyes, including you). But make sure you end with a positive statement, such as "You know I still love you, and this behavior won't change my opinion of you" (even if you threatened to stab the stuffed panda and five classmates with scissors).

If a student shows remorse or apologizes, share the forgiveness God gives us in Christ Jesus. You might say, "Everyone makes mistakes, but God forgives you for Jesus' sake. Because He forgives me when I make mistakes, I forgive you too, in His name." Modeling forgiveness helps students learn to offer it to others.

Strategy 4: Encourage good behavior.

Keep an eye out and lavishly praise students when they follow your rules. Verbally point out those times when students listen and do things well. Your affirmation becomes all the more poignant to those who previously felt your wrath . . . errr . . . righteous anger.

Verbally noticing positive behavior also helps during transitions. When students hear you acknowledge someone else's behavior, they want you to notice them doing something good too. Consider using comments like these to offer individual attention and prompt others to join in.

- ◆ *I see Silas and Alex cleaning up.*
- ◆ *Liam's group started working.*
- ◆ *Aisha and Carlo are working hard.*
- ◆ *Isabella and Sophia are ready to hear presentations.*
- ◆ *Welcome to the circle, Aiden.*
- ◆ *I noticed that Kyle already has his markers.*
- ◆ *Ava's here and ready to start a new activity.*

Continue acknowledging behaviors until everyone complies. You might even name every person as he or she joins the new task.

Students frequently sit in school all day and get rebuked for chatting, moving around, not finishing assignments, or failing to focus. This strategy gives you opportunity to speak children's names in positive tones, reinforce behaviors, and encourage individuals. You can become a refreshing source of encouragement in students' lives. Don't miss this joy!

Strategy 5: Follow up.

If needed, set a follow-up time to make sure your student made appropriate changes to his or her behavior. Use this time to build a stronger relationship with this student. This bond will most likely prevent that particular problem from happening again, and it keeps the door open for correcting future bad behavior in a loving and understanding manner.

Working with your biggest goofballs

They interrupted every single lesson I ever taught, knocked object lessons off tables, and peppered my heartfelt speeches with silly comments at all the wrong times.

I constantly found their ridiculous comments written all over my office. They drew strange pictures of me, including one where I resembled a super-hero covered in tattoos, for no discernible reason. They persisted with one creative prank after another.

They wreaked havoc on the air mattresses during mission trips, tossed ketchup packets in restaurants, and threw water bottles at the back of my head.

In other words, they were my resident goofballs.

And as much as I still love them, I wholeheartedly agree with the phrase a fellow leader once uttered about them: "They can drive even the strongest youth leader to tears in under ten minutes."

Although they never personally drove me to such a brink of emotion, I learned a lot about the personality of goofball kids. As with all people, there's more to these zany students than meets the eye.

Intent on getting to the bottom of these wild minds, I sat down and inter-viewed two of the biggest goofballs I know, Jake and Joey. I sought the true confessions of a total goofball from these now-college-age teens. Some of their answers surprised even me.

First of all, why do these kids act so foolishly? According to Jake, "I like to make people laugh, and I enjoy making people happy. If you can make someone laugh, you're in for a 'friend ticket.'"

Joey spoke more frankly. "I act goofy because I don't want to be boring. I like to have a dramatic life, where no day is the same day to day. I like to have a reason to get up each morning. If you're not goofy, then you're just normal."

In the opinion of both boys, they earned "class clown" designations at a young age.

"I was labeled as a class clown from kindergarten on, actually, probably from when I came out of the womb, to be honest," cracked Jake. "But I've never really gotten in serious trouble for it. I've never gotten called to the office unless I was constantly annoying. Sure, I goof off for the first few hours of class, but at the right time, I focus on the things around me. But I incorporate laughter into it."

According to Joey, "I used to sit in class and play card games when I was seven or eight. The teachers would walk by and get mad at me, and I would just keep playing. That was the beginning of my goofiness. When I eventually started wearing odd things to school, like duct tape, people really realized that I was a goofball. It became obvious."

According to my two goofballs, their friends and classmates treat them according to their silly social status. "I know people think I get egged on by their laughter, which is true. Sometimes people ignore me, especially girls, but guys usually join in and participate," said Jake.

"People tend to put gas on the fire and let it go," Joey admitted. "They aren't negative but really encourage me to keep on doing what I'm doing."

Is there any way to avoid setting off a goofball? Well, it might be a futile effort, no matter how carefully you tread.

Jake confessed, "If I hear something that sounds like a movie quote, it's an instant trigger. I try to pay attention to teachers and leaders, but sometimes when someone's talking, especially if someone is giving a speech, I can't help but make fun of them."

"Try keeping kids focused," said Joey. "I believe that if you find something that is time-consuming and positive, like sports, you focus more and avoid being goofy. But it's impossible to keep me from acting like a goofball. Try to keep me busy and keep me from being bored, but expect that my goofiness will come out no matter what."

When you find yourself dealing with the inevitable goofball in your ministry, keep in mind that most adults react in one of two ways, according to Jake. "Adults either react back angrily, or they laugh it off."

Joey pointed out that many adults are clueless. "When I was younger, adults really looked down on me and thought I had issues. Now that I'm older, adults either go along with it and joke around, or they're totally oblivious to what's going on and don't even realize what I'm doing."

What's their preference on how adults handle them, even if they're annoyed? Joey admitted he doesn't really care. "I don't care how they react, because if I'm enjoying myself, I think that's all that matters."

However, adults can make goofballs grin. "I love it when adults try to mock me, especially when they try to imitate the annoying action that I've done. It helps refocus me onto what I should pay attention to," Jake said.

What advice would these teens give to adults and leaders who are trying to work with goofballs?

"Realize that I'm really immature. Be strict. Don't be afraid to hurt my feelings. I need you to lay the law down for me. I need rules, and I need punishment," said Jake. "Whenever I do something wrong, I know it, and I generally feel scared and know I need to straighten up right away."

Joey added, "If you plan engaging activities where we won't get bored, like activities where we're building something or drawing something, not just watching a video or talking, I'm more likely to actually pay attention and focus."

Of course, leaders can practice "speaking the truth in love" (Ephesians 4:15) as we guide our precocious students through these formative years. Jake shared, "You don't need to be a jerk about it, but don't be afraid to enforce rules and expectations with me."

Jake readily admitted, "There's a misconception of me as a goofball that I am constantly trying to make people like me. That's not true. I know people like me for who I am, and I also know that I'll grow up and grow out of my immaturity. This 'nonsense destructive stage' will end eventually. But I'm still going to have fun and quote movies and be a normal person, just with a stronger sense of humor than your average person."

Interestingly, Joey agrees. "The more mature I become, the less I'll be a goofball, but it'll never go away completely. It's always going to be with me, but it'll be a smaller part of me. I picture myself sitting in a cubicle someday, cracking jokes and making fun of things, but not in quite the same way I do now."

When asked how they would handle the younger versions of themselves in youth group, both paused for thought.

Jake spoke first. "I think I would probably confront the younger version of me and explain that while I understand you're having fun, you can't disrupt others. I would also make sure to be clear that there are punishments for my continued bad behavior. I need boundaries. And I need someone to punish me when I cross those boundaries."

Joey offered practical ideas as well. "I'd make sure I was doing what I was supposed to but having fun with it. I'd make sure that what I make the younger version of me do is appropriate for my attitude and that it's fun but that there's nothing distracting around. If I had to take items away, playing the Behavior Game as I take items one by one, I'd do it."

So, what's the most important thing for a leader to keep in mind as they work with goofballs?

According to Jake, "Have a sense of humor, but let me know that you're in charge. Don't expect me to listen to you if you just throw out meaningless threats. I need accountability, and I need a leader that can stand up to me and have a backbone."

Joey advised leaders to get to know their goofballs and seek to understand them. "As a leader, it's important to keep in mind that your students are their own person. Make sure that your expectations are appropriate for me. For instance, you wouldn't want to put an irresponsible goofball with infants. But if you understand that I'm a social person, that social outlets are perfect for me, you can assign me activities and jobs that I can fulfill socially."

As much of a handful as your goofballs can be, the Holy Spirit still impacts their lives in tremendous ways.

"My youth leaders were definitely a huge part of my life," said Jake. "In middle school, there was a lot of tough stuff to handle—drugs, sex, temptations. I know that my youth leaders were a lifeline for me. I looked forward to going to church and participating in youth nights every single week. I was able to be friends with my leaders, and I knew that youth nights weren't the only nights I could rely on them, that they cared about me all the time."

What sort of effect does your ministry have on even your goofiest teens? As Jake explained, "Through middle school, I learned that you may think that you've seen it all spiritually, that God isn't so great, that you don't need Him in your life, but you haven't seen it all. There's a bigger picture out there, and we have a God who is really at work."

To Joey, adolescence was a time of learning godly discipline. "Being involved in ministry taught me how to control myself more and think through my decisions and actions. If I was going to be goofy, I learned how to not hurt someone, a more Christian attitude. I learned how to be a goofy Christian, per se."

Both Jake and Joey had powerful faith experiences in youth group.

"My relationship with Jesus has grown so much, even through the simplest devotions and Bible verses we discussed, which spoke to my life in ways that sermons couldn't always do," Jake said. "Through middle school ministry at my church, I came to realize that Christ is my Savior and that I can share that with everyone I meet."

Joey agreed, adding, "I grew in my relationship with Jesus, and I met a lot of good Christian friends. We were able to spend a lot of time together. I learned how Jesus died on the cross for us, and how God loves us enough to send Him to us. I now see God as real family, someone I can talk to without any hesitation."

I've been privileged to see these two goofballs mature into young men and become evangelists. They serve as leaders together in a homeless ministry. They started creative ministries such as a mall outreach where they weekly gather students to walk through the local malls, regularly meet store employees and customers, pray with them, and share the hope of Jesus with them.

As Joey said, "It's pretty amazing! Sometimes mall workers get transferred, but in the three or four weeks we are able to connect, we're able to read the Bible with them and talk about it with them."

Through this mall ministry, Joey has seen God work in incredible ways. "We met several atheists once, and we talked to them for a long time. We encouraged them to get into the Bible and read it. Eventually two of them became Christians and now attend our church."

Section 3

As Jake explained, "I've been a goofball for a long time, but I feel so blessed that I'm not shy with people. I can go up to anyone and talk to them now about my faith. I've gone downtown with our homeless ministry and talked with junkies, and I've seen the Holy Spirit at work."

So, in moments when you're pulling out your hair, trying to keep your biggest goofballs from jumping off furniture and eating your object lessons, remember the insights from these two goofballs. They may not be able to keep their sarcastic comments to themselves, but Scripture and the message of Christ's forgiveness and love can still soak into their hearts.

And remember, too, their faith is as vitally important as anyone else's, even if they're trying to throw Bibles through a basketball hoop. (Boundary alert!)

Girls vs. guys:
what you really need to know

I used to make serious money cashing in on dares from my male friends.

I let my guy friends mix up anything they wanted in a glass. If they paid me, I'd drink it. In vain attempts to make me sick, guys combined chocolate, chili, horseradish, hot sauce, and all sorts of disgusting ingredients in a cup. Without fail, I swallowed it and earned my cash.

Obviously, I grew up as a tomboy. I arm wrestled and flicked paper footballs across the classroom with the best of them. Even as an adult, I prefer a vigorous political debate over kitchen gossip, and I would rather go to a hockey game than paint my nails.

Imagine my chagrin as a young youth leader when I found myself in the midst of a small group of cheerleaders and volleyball players, gabbing about crushes and lipstick and shoes. My giggling, giddy group of seventh graders breezed right past our scheduled ending time and just kept talking. And talking. When I finally forced the girls out of the room, they stopped cooing and wrapped me in a group hug to say good-bye.

It felt like I was dealing with an entirely different species than the careless, carefree boys I grew up with.

The complex differences between men and women are fodder for life's great amusement. Are our differences from hard wiring or from how we raise each gender? Nature or nurture? I'm not throwing my hat in either ring.

Besides, if I had any definitive answers, I'd permanently tour the country, lecturing parents and teachers from sunup to sundown.

Instead, I can share only bits of wisdom about gender differences gleaned from my own experiences. After all, leaders need to understand, appreciate, and consider how to best approach both genders.

Keep in mind that these are general guidelines, and plenty of kids will fall outside of the boundaries of their gender on many of these points.

talk a lot
early complex
vocabulary
value relationships
**want & need
a best friend**
social
deep desire to be loved
fine motor skills excel early
study faces and body actions
praise efforts not looks

GIRLS ····· VERSUS ····· GUYS

high drive for action
competitive
physical &
loud
struggle to
sit and listen
need frequent breaks
**value teams &
working together**
deep desire to be respected
large motor skills excel early
enjoy crowds

Art © Shutterstock, Inc.

The wonder of girls

An old adage proclaims that girls talk, while boys walk.

As many tired parents could attest, it sometimes seems that girls never stop talking. Throughout their lives, females talk three times more than their male counterparts. They exhibit more-complex vocabularies at a younger age. Social interactions matter more to girls, even at a young age. Research shows that female babies study faces and body language more intently than boys.

Girls tend to excel in fine-motor tasks in the first several years of life. Girls manipulate toys and objects faster, drink from cups and use eating utensils sooner, and typically write, and usually more neatly, before boys.

In general, it's helpful to give girls an abundance of words of encouragement and kindness, as long as they are genuine and not syrupy, superficial adoration.

Praising effort rather than looks is one of the most helpful encouragements leaders can offer girls. By recognizing when female students work hard, we reinforce positive and productive behavior that becomes a foundation in their lives.

From a young age through adulthood, girls deeply desire to know that they're loved and beautiful. Little girls talk about handsome knights rescuing princesses because it speaks to a real longing in their heart, a wish to know someone values them enough to fight for them.

Those who work with girls need to understand this strong need for love and acceptance, and share that our worth comes from our identity in Christ. Modeling confidence as a child of God positively connects with girls.

We want to raise confident women who adapt to whatever comes their way in life. Society often unfairly labels a confident young lady as conceited or difficult. We must remind girls to appreciate and use their God-given strengths with humility and trust in the Lord. Girls need to know we commit to them for the long haul.

Even from a young age, girls value relationships deeply. Often, this becomes the source of adolescent friendship angst and drama. Girls place high significance on having a confidant, someone they can talk to about anything. Because of this, female mentors can influence the emotional, social, mental, and spiritual development of a young girl tremendously.

One of the most challenging things about working with girls is understanding the dark world of female aggression. Girls typically bully one another emotionally, utilizing subtle tactics such as social exclusion, gossip, manipulation, and verbal attacks. Trite remarks and snide comments often hurt feelings. Most girls wrestle with a "frenemy," a friend who acts as an enemy, from grade school through adulthood.

Since girls highly prize relationships, any breakdown in a friendship can trigger a massive breach in a girl's well-being. Thus, though friend drama may seem petty and insignificant to adults, it can rock the world of a young girl. As you work with girls, gently support them as they inevitably pour out their woes to you.

Teach girls to speak and act honestly. Encourage them to stand up for themselves, as well as for others who get bullied. When you see female aggression, whether gossip or exclusion, swiftly nip it in the bud with proper severity that ensures your students understand it's unacceptable.

Listen to girls with genuine interest. Reflect observations back to them that you notice about their likes and passions. See if you can find out what makes them light up with joy. By the time puberty sets in during the middle school years, girls experience a tremendous amount of stress as they deal with changing bodies, new schools, higher academic and social demands, and raucous emotions all at once.

Adults can benefit young ladies by giving perspective by sharing their own stories of how they survived difficult times. When girls understand others shared their struggles and survived, they usually start to see a light at the end of the tunnel.

The joy of boys

When I think about working with boys, I picture the many times I watched middle school boys gleefully wrestle one another to the ground and pretend to pummel one another, all while smiling.

Even from infancy, boys tend to be more physical and action oriented. They take great delight in crawling, then toddling, running, and climbing over virtually everything in sight. Whereas girls focus on relationships and social interactions, boys pay attention to activity.

According to a study by psychologists at the University of Cambridge, when given the choice of looking at people talking or windshield wipers moving, twelve-month-old boys chose to watch the wipers. (*Human Sex Differences in Social and Non-Social Looking Preferences, at 12 Months of Age,* Simon Baron-Cohen and Svetlana Lutchmaya, © December 2002 *Infant Behavior and Development,* University of Cambridge.)

Leaders often fear boys will destroy everything or accidentally injure themselves—or perhaps achieve both in the same swift move.

With such high drive for action, boys often struggle to sit still and listen. Leaders need to instill this foundational behavior in young students, as its mastery carries lifelong repercussions.

Keep in mind, though, that boys need frequent movement and action breaks in their schedules. Giving time to run around, toss a toy, or bounce a ball helps boys manage their energetic young bodies. Don't be alarmed by physical tussling, but quickly step in if the playful cuffing becomes more aggressive. Young boys need to learn the difference between good-natured ribbing and outright abuse.

A deep desire for respect drives boys. Playground boasts about sports achievements or running faster than others indicate the drive for others to notice them and their capabilities. Boys hone confidence by achieving many goals they vigorously tackle. And make no mistake, men are challenge oriented from infancy through adulthood. They love goals and usually work diligently to achieve them.

Leaders need to remember how sincerely boys love competition. Whereas girls value relationships and sometimes shy away from rivalry, boys love to get into the nitty-gritty of a physical or mental throwdown. When working with male students, try engaging them in debates, athletic feats, and small contests.

In moments when boys seem bored, put the lesson on pause and spend a few minutes reinvigorating their lagging interest with a physical challenge. I once stopped a lesson with drooling teen boys, threw my marker across the large room, and said that the first one to grab it and bring it back to me won. Before the words were even out of my mouth, the boys leapt out of their chairs and fought happily over the marker. Within the span of a minute, they settled back in their chairs, alert and invigorated for the rest of the lesson.

Boys love a good crowd. Research shows that male newborns prefer to look at a mobile of faces rather than a single face. Men value a team and enthusiastically throw themselves into working together toward a common goal. For the same reason, they often swear loyalty to a professional or collegiate sports team and avidly follow it.

In comparison with girls, less conflict occurs among boys when we lump them together. In general, boys tend to be much louder and more active than their female counterparts.

Though boys express their feelings less often than girls, they still battle insecurities. They don't always feel as fearless or brave as they try to act.

Males need strong male role models to look up to and imitate as they progress from rambunctious boys to men. They must be taught to value God and follow His directives for their life rather than adhere to the worldly definitions of success. Challenge them to speak and act honestly, as truthful men of integrity who care for those around them.

While you won't get many face-to-face emotional conversations with boys, take opportunities to talk to them as you work together side by side. These kinds of conversations foster deep kinship in the boys who play video games or sports together.

We need each other

Despite the differences between males and females, both genders need each other. As Galatians 3:28 poignantly reminds us, "There is neither Jew nor Greek, there is neither slave nor free, there is no male and female, for you are all one in Christ Jesus."

God favors no gender, nationality, or social status over another. The blood of Jesus covers the sins of the world (John 1:29; 3:16; 1 Timothy 2:6). The Holy Spirit working through God's Word and Sacraments shows us this truth and gives us faith in Christ. We receive forgiveness of sins and become part of Christ's Body, the Church.

However, in mentor situations, it's always wise to pair women with girls and men with boys. People usually relate better to role models they perceive as similar to themselves. Each gender benefits greatly from interacting with the other, but same-gender relationships offer more value for role modeling and empathetic sharing as teens develop identities and establish societal roles.

Remember that whether you work with males or females, each gender possesses its own challenges and joys. Roll with the punches and focus on the advantageous qualities in your students. Instead of merely basing your expectations of individuals on what you think about boys and girls, seek awareness of each child's unique personality, disposition, and talents. Focus on developing them in positive directions.

Helpful tips for teaching in the real world

You might be tempted to think I'm a hippie for saying this, but I love mixing paint.

Come on, the kindergarten version of you would agree with me, right?

As weird as you may now think I am, I absolutely love mixing a few daubs of color together and twirling them around with a paintbrush until a new color develops. There's something calming about watching these colors harmonize and blend into one solid hue.

While I'm at it, I might as well clear the air about my other weird quirks too. I brush my teeth in the shower and absolutely loathe wearing socks. Go ahead, judge away.

In the same way I marvel at the practice of swirling paint together to make a new color, I inexplicably love teaching and seeing a new experience blend into the brain of another person to create a richer, more vibrant individual.

When it comes to teaching, I humbly bow at the feet of many bright experts who know much more than I do. I've read many excellent books and articles on education, and I encourage you to do so as well. Take advantage of the loads of knowledge out there.

Many talented people have written tips for teaching different age groups. I'll share only the "cheat sheet" tips that remain most important to my job and probably most helpful to you. I hope they help you get a good grasp of children's physical, social, emotional, intellectual, and spiritual capabilities.

Working with small children (babies through preschool)

What's going on with them?

PHYSICALLY

- *Developing from the head down to their toes, starting with their heads*
- *Growing rapidly and need plenty of rest in between spurts of great activity*
- *Very little muscle control and are just learning small-muscle coordination*

SOCIALLY

◆ *Self-focused and incapable of seeing another's perspective*

◆ *In our eyes, going through what we would call a stage of "selfishness" as they consider their own needs primary over anything else*

◆ *Tend to feel insecure around strangers and in new situations*

EMOTIONALLY

◆ *A great love for exploration and discovery*

◆ *Love repetition*

◆ *Find security in routine and patterns*

INTELLECTUALLY

◆ *Learn through experiences; starting to express curiosity*

◆ *Question everything around them*

◆ *Very limited understanding of space and awareness of time; unable to comprehend chronology*

◆ *Short attention spans, generally one minute per year of age*

SPIRITUALLY

◆ *Beginning to form a concept of God*

◆ *Starting to learn to talk freely about God*

◆ *Learning the basics of right and wrong and how God views actions and attitudes*

Five things to remember at all times

◆ **Use appropriate materials.**

Choosing the right toys, games, and furniture and defining play areas are literally a matter of life and death. Because this age group explores everything around them with insatiable curiosity, it's imperative to surround them with safe learning equipment.

Providing a large, clean, and safe space small children can explore offers mental stimulation they crave.

Remember, these kids primarily use their bodies to explore, so expect them to put items in their mouth, grab them with tiny hands, and climb all over them.

◆ *Alternate between activity and rest.*

Small children vacillate between periods of intense energy and rest. Use many different learning activities and experiences. Teach to all the senses. They need to touch, taste, feel, hear, and smell items as their tiny brains develop. Give many opportunities for rest, as they tire quickly and need time to recharge.

◆ *Provide consistency.*

Most small children tend to feel timid about new situations and unsure of new caregivers, whether teenagers or adults. To ease apprehension, provide consistent leaders and patterns for their experiences.

For instance, if small children see the same friendly faces each week and know your class always opens with a song or a prayer, they are more likely to relax. Routines and schedules make them feel safe and secure.

◆ *Explain to little minds.*

Keep young, developing brains at the forefront of your mind as you plan time together. Small children understand things from only their personal perspective, and they have very short attention spans.

Emphasize the present, because they don't comprehend the concepts of past or future. Steer clear of referencing things that they never experienced or won't experience until they're older. Instead, focus on the sorts of things they encounter on a daily basis.

◆ *Keep it simple.*

Use simple questions and answers in your lessons with these little guys. Avoid complex examples.

Small children don't need a lot of details or history. Focus your lessons on one main point and provide clear, simple, repetitive answers throughout your time together.

Section 3

Working with elementary children (kindergarten through grade school)

What's going on with them?

PHYSICALLY

◆ *Muscles are becoming more coordinated. They're "growing into" their bodies and usually get taller by the year.*

◆ *Kids perform tasks with greater energy and enthusiasm.*

◆ *They want to hone physical skills that show their increased coordination, such as writing, sketching, and physical games, such as baseball and soccer.*

SOCIALLY

◆ *Social skills expand as kids explore concepts of friendship.*

◆ *Tend to have friendships along gender lines (boys with boys, girls with girls)*

◆ *Many skirmishes about fairness*

EMOTIONALLY

◆ *An increased desire for acceptance leads to the pursuit of positive group interactions.*

◆ *Many children enjoy the idea of clubs or groups because of their keen interest in group involvement.*

◆ *Feelings become hurt more easily. Children desire empathy.*

INTELLECTUALLY

◆ *Attention spans are growing but remain fairly short.*

◆ *Children think literally and concretely. They need straightforward lessons with many examples.*

◆ *Memory is sharp, so they love to memorize all sorts of things.*

◆ *Enjoy learning creatively*

◆ *Like to collect things and dabble in many different hobbies, not just one main focus*

SPIRITUALLY

- *Listen carefully to the beliefs of key adults and teachers and adopt these beliefs as their own*
- *Beginning to see how Scripture connects with them personally*
- *Can grasp a basic sense of faith and how it affects their lives*

Five things to remember at all times

- **Gear toward their developing intellect.**

  As these young minds continue to grow, satisfy their endlessly buzzing brains by providing bountiful activities and information. These kids are spongelike in their ability to absorb knowledge about many different things. They easily memorize, and this can be a great time to teach Scripture memorization.

- **Encourage friendship.**

  Friendship can be an all-consuming passion for elementary-age children. Their social skills are still growing, so although they have a deep desire for relationships, they don't always know how to manage friendships appropriately.

  Generally, friendships form along gender lines, with kids preferring to spend most of their time in same-gender groups. Provide plenty of opportunities for positive group interaction, because these are foundational years to hone social skills.

  Manage inevitable relationship conflicts swiftly before they turn into bigger dramas. Give empathy to the small battles that burden these little hearts.

- **Teach creatively.**

  This age group adores creative lessons, so practice a variety of different learning experiences. They enjoy many illustrations and examples, and they like to give input when asked.

  Keep in mind that young kids think concretely and literally, so don't get caught teaching with a lot of symbolism, abstract theories, or comparing items with "like" language.

◆ *Give outlets for growing bodies.*

Elementary kids' muscles are still developing. They grow rapidly, at varying rates. Energy levels are higher than ever, and they feel excited to engage in physical challenges.

By making activities into games and skill challenges, you easily hook them into focusing on a subject.

◆ *Be positive.*

Kids this age wrestle with the growing complexities of relationships. Friendship and peer interaction are daily challenges. We must allow them to learn to navigate safely. When they make mistakes, we need to show optimism, encouragement, and empathy.

Elementary students are highly attuned to a belittling, mocking attitude from people older than them, so treat their feelings with appropriate sensitivity and gentle respect.

Working with preadolescents (middle school)

What's going on with them?

PHYSICALLY

◆ *Going through serious, rapid growth spurts and puberty*

◆ *Worry more about appearance (and acne) as their bodies become more adult-like*

◆ *Muscle development progresses and becomes more refined.*

◆ *Starting to be attracted to the opposite sex, but unsure of how to handle it*

◆ *Energy levels are higher than ever.*

SOCIALLY

◆ *Increased importance of friends and popularity, with increasing influence of peers*

◆ *Deep concern over appearance and social standing*

◆ *Desire to become more independent and understand their identity*

◆ *Enjoy connecting with adults and role models, especially one-on-one*

EMOTIONALLY

◆ *Becoming more expressive about emotions*

◆ *Emotions fluctuate wildly, causing emotional roller coasters.*

◆ *Struggle with self-esteem*

◆ *Love personal attention from friends and adults alike*

◆ *Increasingly adventurous spirit tempered by fear of failure*

◆ *Desire increased freedom*

INTELLECTUALLY

◆ *Transitioning from concrete to abstract thinking*

◆ *Idealistic and often overly ambitious about tackling challenges*

◆ *Just starting to develop problem-solving skills with growing reasoning ability*

◆ *Beginning to vocalize their own opinions*

◆ *Starting to question what they've been taught, addressing significant questions in their lives*

SPIRITUALLY

◆ *Beginning to question the faith of their childhood and make it their own rather than just accept what they heard from parents or other adults*

◆ *Resonate with the idea of their identity being found in Christ and as God's children*

◆ *Starting to apply spiritual principles to their daily lives*

◆ *Look for ways to act on and experience what they learned*

Five things to remember at all times

◆ ***Set expectations and keep them.***

Middle schoolers will always try to test your boundaries, to see how far they can push you. Don't let their constant nagging change your decisions. Aim high and they'll respond.

Be firm in the way you handle your group. They will walk all over you if you let them, so be assertive in your leadership. Hold them to your expectations, such as cleaning up the classroom if they made a mess.

Section 3

Preadolescents balance the tension between childhood and adulthood, and they need strong guidance in this tricky journey.

◆ **Create a safe environment.**

Young teenagers need to feel safe and unthreatened so they can open up and share the many worries on their hearts. Utilize methods that allow students to vocalize beliefs, opinions, and feelings in constructive ways. Help guide them through their emotional highs and lows, and seriously address their questions and doubts.

Since they deal with many physical and emotional changes, they don't like games or activities that single them out. Avoid doing things that draw attention to individuals, involve speed or strength, or make kids nervous beforehand.

They need to feel comfortable while working through their issues, so plan your room carefully. If possible, avoid having kids sit formally at desks. Instead, consider a semicircle of beanbags on the floor. Use a youth room or other informal area.

◆ **Be authentic.**

This age responds well to a diverse mix of leaders: parents, high school and college students, young adults, and older adults. They realize adults had different experiences than they do. They relate better when you show humility and willingly share some of your embarrassing moments, not just your accomplishments. Let them laugh at you.

They really treasure time you spend with them. They realize you invest time and energy in them, and they appreciate it, even if they won't tell you that!

◆ **Vary activities.**

Because individuals grow and change rapidly at different rates, an activity that one student might like may repulse another. Plan diverse activities, keep a fast pace in your sessions, and remember that middle schoolers can focus for an average of ten to fourteen minutes at a time before their attention wanes.

Include many experiences to provide something for everyone during your time together. Include activities that let all kids participate, not just one individual.

Change pace frequently, and break up the routine with music, conversation, handouts, movement, and games. Young teens learn best through kinesthetic activities, where they actually do things. "Living lessons" are much more effective than lectures.

◆ **Connect personally.**

Intentionally connecting with middle schoolers makes a world of difference to them and how they respond to you. Try to connect with each teen personally, outside of class. Talk to them at church or the grocery store. If you send them a postcard or a text, they treasure it.

These teens often feel alone in their journey to adulthood. They begin bumping heads with their parents, so they welcome attention from other adults.

Working with teenagers (high school)

What's going on with them?

PHYSICALLY

◆ *Physical development hits hard, especially for boys, as students fill out and resemble adults.*

◆ *Boys generally take longer to feel comfortable with their new bodies and are often awkward or clumsy as they adjust.*

◆ *Sexuality and the expression of it become a major focus.*

SOCIALLY

◆ *Challenged with conflicting feelings, especially a desire for independence versus a strong desire to be part of a group*

◆ *Friendship becomes incredibly important; teens align themselves with a friend group.*

◆ *Friend groups have major impact on identity and decisions.*

◆ *Authority becomes a difficult issue, especially with parents, as teens struggle to internalize authority in order to become functional young adults.*

EMOTIONALLY

◆ *Identity and personality become all-absorbing concerns.*

◆ *Teens become generally assertive with their identity, even though they may not think through all the implications of a newly assumed one.*

◆ *Self-absorbed thoughts consume the adolescent brain.*

◆ *Teens develop attachments to beliefs, values, and elements of personal style that link them with others of similar beliefs.*

INTELLECTUALLY

◆ *Interpersonal perspective changes, as students become more aware of how others see them and respond to those perceptions.*

◆ *Reasoning skills and understanding of abstract thoughts sharpen as formal operational thinking begins.*

◆ *Students begin to think their own thoughts, not just believe what they're told.*

◆ *Teens enjoy reflecting on their own stories and making things personal.*

SPIRITUALLY

◆ *For the first time, faith becomes highly personal and important.*

◆ *Self-absorption with faith leads to an increased interest in hearing personal faith stories and testimonies.*

◆ *Since teens want independence, they want to choose their own faith. But since their experience is limited and they want to be a part of a group, they usually tend to follow the faith of their parents or close friends.*

◆ *With increased abstract thought, students start to piece together stories into one larger story and understand the context of faith.*

Five things to remember at all times

◆ ***Don't talk down to them.***

One of the biggest frustrations countless teenagers have confided to me is how much they hate when people talk down to them, treating them like they're stupid little kids. Teens are keenly aware of the slightest hint of superiority, and it shrivels their spirits faster than a ripe tomato in the hot summer sun.

Remember, they desire independence, and they struggle with authority. Treat them with respect and, when in doubt, more like an adult than like a child.

Because adolescents are intrinsically self-focused, don't alienate them by minimizing their feelings. Saying things like "That's not a big deal" and "Just wait until you grow up" and "You're too young to understand" shuts them down.

◆ *Embrace tough topics.*

Today's teenagers face a daily deluge of incredibly deep, complex issues. Allow them to think, explore, discuss, and express doubts or questions in a safe and nonjudgmental way. Be real, open, and honest.

Don't be afraid to talk about controversial things. Someone needs to talk about it with them; it's better you, a caring and Christ-centered individual, than a stranger online.

Even though you do not know all the answers, don't shy away from tackling challenging subject matter. Your willingness to navigate choppy waters side by side extends a lifeline to their hearts. Show what you believe through your actions and words. Let them see and hear your beliefs.

◆ *Be understanding.*

Sharing personal stories and struggles offers many benefits because teenagers appreciate honesty and authenticity. They're very interested in personal testimonies, and they are often fascinated about why you want to work with them. This offers a great opportunity to share about your motivation to love as Christ loves you.

However, we need to remember that our experience is not their experience. Avoid comparing your own high school experience with theirs, as it tends to frustrate them. They think you couldn't possibly understand the troubles they face. Today's kids live in a very different world. Seek to understand their world without judging, and admit when you don't know something about them or their culture.

Be very sensitive regarding gender also. In general, because teens struggle with understanding more mature emotions, men should mentor high school boys and women should mentor high school girls.

◆ *Encourage them.*

This generation needs caring guidance more than ever, so take every opportunity to speak the truth in love and encourage them. Confidentiality is important, but be highly aware of when topics become too sensitive or require help you do not have expertise to handle.

If you discover that a student harms or threatens to harm himself or others, battles neglect or abuse, or deals with severe mental or emotional issues, seek appropriate outside assistance immediately to keep the student, his family, and friends safe.

Often, a teenager prefaces these sensitive topics with phrases like "Swear you won't tell anyone before I tell you this." I recommend responding, "I'll keep this confidential unless I think someone might be in danger and I would need to share it in order to help that person. If that happens, I'll let you know first before I tell someone else, so we can work through it together."

This establishes that you are open to listening and helping, but it doesn't bind you to silence if someone genuinely needs help.

◆ *Allow opportunities for autonomy.*

The transition to adulthood from childhood challenges all teenagers. Adolescents feel confused about how they fit into the world. They desire independence, but most experience limited self-sufficiency. Giving teens plenty of opportunities for leadership and autonomy launches them into safe navigation of something that often seems daunting and scary.

Access their regular freedoms to great benefit by asking students to take on responsibilities. For example, ask students to collect attendance, assist with a demonstration, lead a portion of the discussion or a small group, support other teen leaders, pick topics or curriculum, or help plan events.

Vary directed activities and discussions. Give teens a chance to step into self-sufficiency whenever you can.

Teaching Tricks

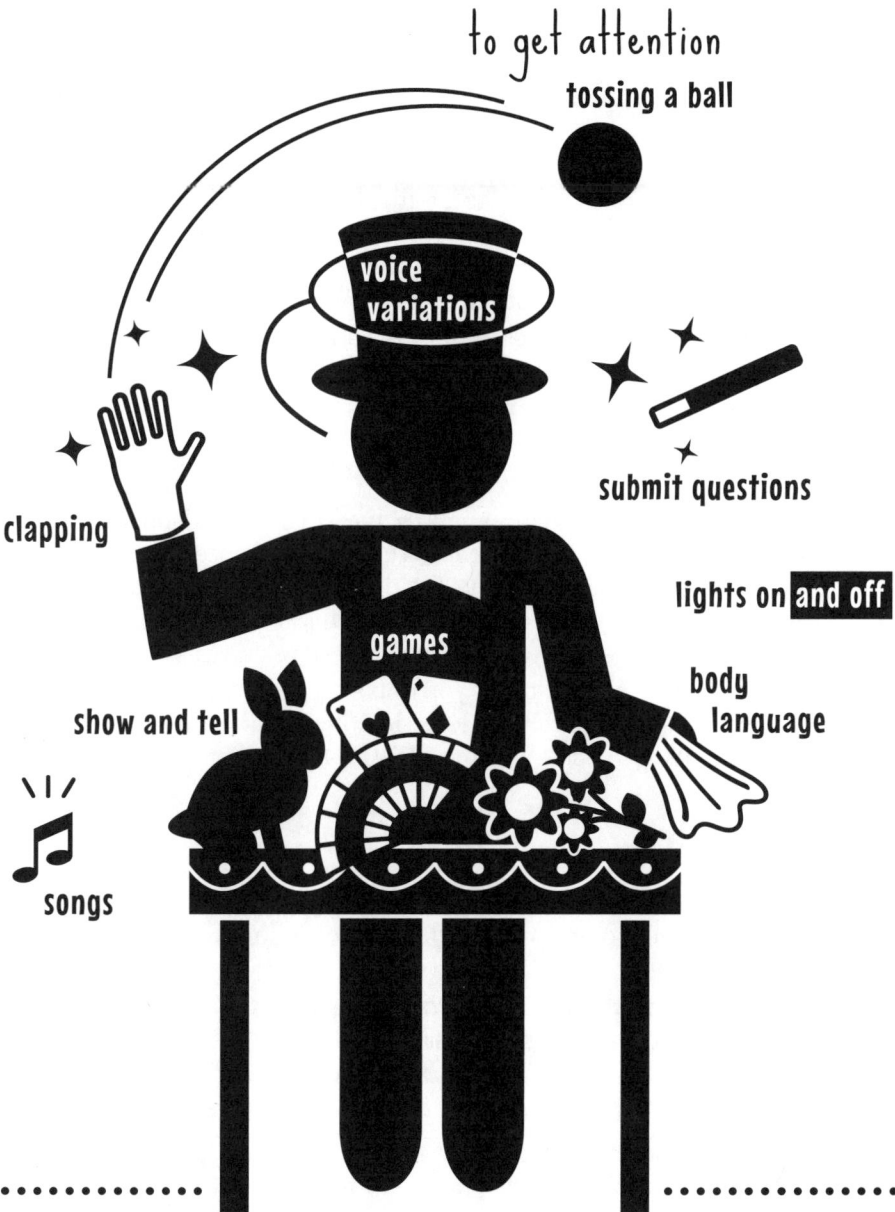

to get attention

tossing a ball

voice variations

submit questions

clapping

lights on **and off**

games

body language

show and tell

songs

Tricks that work for all ages

The first time I was in charge of a class of five-year-olds, I broke out in a cold sweat.

I kid you not.

All those little faces stared up at me, wide-eyed and silent. In contrast to the teenagers I constantly battled into submission, these tiny human creatures didn't put up a fight. They sat down without even asking them twice. They waited patiently. They watched me like a hawk. It freaked me out.

Eventually, my class of too-good-to-be-true kiddos ended up being just as unpredictable and challenging as teenagers, albeit in different ways. Though they started as quiet and attentive angels, they eventually needed reining in plenty of times over the course of our time together.

Many years of teaching all ages, toddlers to adults, taught me some clever techniques to grab the attention of students, no matter their age.

These are go-to tricks I use on a regular basis.

Clapping

A student taught me a simple auditory trick I call the Clapping Game. Stand in front of the group. In a normal voice, say, "Clap once if you can hear me." Students close enough to hear will clap, and the noise itself catches the attention of others. Continue, repeating the command and increasing the number of claps until everyone claps along and listens.

Invite younger students to listen to you clap a specific pattern and repeat it. Continue for a few rounds until they listen intently and focus on your words. Once your students focus and become silent, transition into your lesson or activity.

Lights on and off

Flicking the lights in your room off and on guarantees that everyone freezes in place. Give a quick command or instruction in the brief interlude of silence that follows.

You can use this strategy regularly to establish a visual routine for your group, but it's best to limit its use to maintain its strong effect.

Body language

Using your hands or arms to visually cue students quickly and easily captures the attention of a group. Whether you raise your hand in the air to signal silence, flash a thumbs-up, or put a finger to your lips, choose actions to frequently alert your students.

The key? Don't stop the action until every student looks your way and becomes silent. This trick loses effectiveness if you give up on it while half the group continues talking.

Tossing a ball

By tossing a ball in the air, you catch the attention of your students, especially boys. Inevitably, they want to play with the ball too. For an easy activity, invite them to sit in a circle on the floor. Roll or toss the ball to kids to give them a turn to answer questions. This is a great icebreaker for students of all ages.

You can also make a game out of tossing the ball across the room to someone sitting in their seat and ready to listen. This makes it a surefire way to get everyone to focus quickly.

Show and tell

Hold up an unusual object or picture or play a video clip for a powerful attention-getter. The bigger the display of anticipation you make, the more receptive your students become.

For instance, hiding an object in a paper bag and exclaiming, "Oh boy, I can't even believe I'm going to show you the crazy, dangerous thing I have inside this bag!" definitely hooks attention.

I don't recommend bringing a blowtorch or ninja swords, however. I don't want you telling youth ministry stories from prison.

Submit questions or responses

This method works best for kids who can write. It quickly harnesses the energy of your class in a silent activity.

Invite students to write a question or opinion about a topic. Collect the pieces of paper in a basket and then immediately launch your lesson by reading a few responses aloud. This easily draws students to your topic.

Some students enjoy this activity so much that they want to do it often. I use it with middle school religion classes all year long, inviting them weekly to submit questions for "Ask Anything Fridays." The kids love it because it's engaging, fascinating, and keeps us moving at a fast pace. I love it because they get to ask the inevitable questions ruminating all week long in their young brains. It's a win-win.

Section 3

Voice variations

One trick that works best with younger kids is to quiet your voice to a mere whisper to give commands. As kids notice your lips moving, they stop talking and strain to hear you.

Also try changing the volume of your speech frequently to help students stay more easily engrossed in what you say.

Songs

Using a song to get student attention works well for all ages. Invite younger kids to sing with you. If the song is new, ask them to listen to the words and then sing along.

Play a song for older students and ask them to explain the lyrics. Make sure you tell students to listen in advance, or you'll just pointlessly blast music in an already loud room.

Games

One of the oldest tricks in the book captures attention by inviting students to play a game. Whether it's a quick feat for one or two kids, such as seeing how many pencils a child can balance on the back of her hand, or a lengthy game for the whole class, students show immediate interest in playing a game.

Once you have their attention, take advantage of their zeal by quickly transitioning into your lesson.

Relating to your students

Even now, I can recall the rush of embarrassment I felt as the two girls stood over me, laughing at my math assignment.

Though learning basic addition and subtraction was new and confusing to a seven-year-old, these smug fifth graders cruelly made fun of my homework and called it "ridiculously easy." They loudly proclaimed, "Even a baby could do this math!"

My little face turned red with humiliation as their words cut me to the quick. The damage these careless kids did to me through their cruel jibes was incalculable. I struggled for years to regain the confidence I lost in my math ability. Though they didn't tell me I was stupid, their thoughtless tone and taunts told me exactly what they thought of me.

No doubt you think these girls acted carelessly with a tiny heart. I pray we never harm students, but sometimes words or actions are misunderstood and unknowingly cause damage.

Many people go through a hazy amnesia after high school. They emerge as adults and somehow forget the very real emotions of their life as a child. Adults often glaze over their past, somehow recalling a few highlights but forgetting the general angst of adolescence.

They gloss over the little victories that please children, such as sitting in the front seat of the car or ordering their own meal. They ignore heartaches that burden young shoulders, like having too much history homework or losing a favorite stuffed animal. In short, adult problems loom large in their minds and they forget the troubles they experienced as a child or adolescent.

One of the biggest complaints I hear from students of all ages is that adults make few attempts to understand how they actually feel and what they face. My teenagers identify the most annoying phrase adults say to kids as "You think you have it bad? Let me tell you about my childhood!"

When we carelessly use our words to parade our own challenges as more difficult than the ones children face, we devalue their experiences. And truthfully, these are the most challenging issues our students have ever faced. Without a wealth of life experiences to draw from, every trouble seems insurmountable to them. As their brains continue to form, they experience higher highs and lower lows than adults. A small slight can become a major tragedy. A momentary happiness can become a gigantic joy.

As leaders, we have an incredible opportunity to connect with students in a unique way that most adults don't get. Kids know they need help navigating this confusing world, so they let us in, often more than their own parents. It's imperative that we treat their invitation with gravity and venture into their world without conveying judgment.

Listen and watch what absorbs the attention of your students. View the clips they watch on Vine and YouTube. Listen to their playlists. Watch an episode of one of their favorite shows. Check out their favorite bands. Meet their friends, parents, and guardians. Visit their schools.

Doing these things tells you more about their culture and gives you a glimpse of their world. This information helps you tailor your messages and lessons to them.

When it comes to relating to our students, we must be authentic, genuine, and loving. If we truly consider our ministry to them to be of the utmost importance, we must sometimes sacrifice our egos to fully invest in them.

That means biting back a sarcastic comment about "real trouble" when a child tearfully tells you he lost his favorite yo-yo and the world stopped. It means purposely zipping your lips and letting your students share their feelings and thoughts, even though you may want to tell story after story of your own. It means hiding a smile over what may seem silly or insignificant to you.

Show your students that you enjoy spending time with them, even if you don't particularly feel it that moment. Never make fun of students, to their faces or behind their backs. Spouting sarcastic comments adults consider humorous can deliver a crushing blow to a child. No kid ever wants to hear that she's "a wild little rug rat" or that you need a glass of wine after putting up with his nonsense all day. Speak kindly and compliment them. Speak positively about them to their parents, coaches, and teachers. It makes a difference in how children see you.

I make every attempt to draw my students into conversation. Though I'm an extrovert, I make a concerted effort to guide and facilitate discussions rather than just lecture or share stories from my life. When I teach, I generally talk a quarter of the time. My students talk about 75 percent of the time. Through deep conversation, they often delve into truth they identify as more profound because they stumbled across it themselves, rather than hearing it secondhand from a leader.

Patience is one of the most important qualities needed to work with students. It takes patience to repeat directions multiple times. It takes patience to wait for tiny hands to turn to pages in their Bibles. It takes patience to let students stumble through an activity without doing it for them. It takes patience to help plant the seed of faith in their hearts and not always get to see that seed take root, sprout, and flourish as they grow.

It also takes self-discipline and understanding to put up with students' antics sometimes. Recently, I decided to pay my middle school religion class a compliment about their good behavior. Literally the exact moment I shared a heartfelt message about how they bless me, I saw a male student raise his hand, smack another boy in the side of the head, and beam at me with a giant grin.

Kids are kids, not independent, self-sufficient adults. They don't have our level of self-control, and they need us to model it for them, especially when they make poor decisions.

They may act squirmy and antsy. They have short attention spans. They may complain about everything under the sun, from the temperature of the room to the hardness of their chairs. They can wrestle one another to the ground, poke one another annoyingly for hours on end, and toss paper clips across the room with remarkable accuracy. It takes time to develop a resiliency to their goofiness and frustrating quirks, but if you care about them, you must do it.

We must operate from a place of loving concern. Every moment is an opportunity to teach, whether that means displaying a good attitude even when the bus breaks down or modeling humility when you forget a student's request to cut his sandwich in triangles. Kids won't recall every activity you ever did with them, but they'll remember your heartfelt care for life.

As Maya Angelou once said, "At the end of the day people won't remember what you said or did. They will remember how you made them feel." By the power of the Holy Spirit, may they also remember what we showed, taught, and shared with them about God's Word and His love expressed to us in His Son, Christ Jesus.

Section 3

Get their attention, break the ice, and keep them talking

The smell was the most disgusting thing about it,
once you got past the gray oozing sludge.

As I dramatically posed to take a giant bite out of the spongy Twinkie filled with gooey baby food instead of delicious cream filling, I had the fleeting thought, "I really hope this is worth it. And that my digestive system recovers from this episode of abuse."

I confess to doing many strange things to garner the attention of my youth. Some of the oddest things involved covering kids in frosting and mustard, sliding through a kiddie pool of homemade slime, electrocuting a pickle, getting hit in the face with flour bombs, and even purchasing a live goldfish for an object lesson.

Don't worry, the fish became a pet.

A good leader willingly tries many creative ideas to reach students in powerful new ways. Whether it's a crazy object lesson or unbelievably funny experience, if it opens kids up to laugh, discuss, and ask questions, it benefits your ministry.

Capturing the attention of kids with the creative genius of the Creator, the pure love of our Savior, and the wonderful work of the Holy Spirit is central to my purpose for teaching.

It's pretty simple, really. If our students' ears never tune in to our message, they might completely miss that life-changing, eternity-impacting message of the Gospel.

Frankly, the art of capturing kids' attention is an art. As a skill that comes only through experience, it's difficult to learn from reading or even watching someone else.

You can't just soak up this wisdom by putting your forehead against this book. Kudos to you, though, for laying your head down in frustration rather than bashing it against a wall.

Let me comfort you with the very honest admission that, although I work with kids of all ages for hours a day, I still work to get their attention. Sometimes I hit a perfect note, and kids tune in with rapt attention. Often, I strike out and rack my brain to capture their interest another way. This tricky task challenges even the wisest and most experienced leaders.

So let's get practical and consider how to capture the attention of students so you can share important Gospel truths with them.

First, create a pattern of students tuning in to you.

Tearing students away from their phones, tablets, and chatter with friends can seem daunting unless you establish a clear expectation. As kids in any group setting can readily tell you, phones go away when we focus on God. I share this personal rule the first time a group meets. If I see someone get out a phone, I happily stow it away and don't give it back until the end of the session.

Don't blow my cover with my kids, but I honestly remember taking away only two phones in my entire career. Because I clearly state this expectation and demand their full attention, students honor it. By explaining that I want them to unplug from technology and engage in some good old-fashioned face-to-face time together, they actually value that time away from their gadgets.

Find a way to draw the attention of your students to your teaching space, whether standing on a stage or at the front of a room. I typically holler to my kids to go to their seats and get settled. Giving kids a few moments to collect themselves and get a bit of energy out of their system always helps, so don't fuss about noise levels or activity at this point.

Once you have your students' attention, swoop in like a falcon and dive wholeheartedly into whatever message or activity you planned. Don't waste time on small talk, pointless questions, or readying supplies. Go for the meat. Fully commit. Keep kids from becoming sidetracked.

Lest you miss my point, let me be extremely clear. Kids have way more interesting jokes and juicy tidbits of gossip to share than patience for watching you flounder, stall, and look at your notes for the fourteenth time. Rehearse and polish every opening, making them fascinating enough to engage kids immediately.

Remember to hit a variety of learning styles and strive to use thought-provoking discussion questions. Incorporate many different elements into each lesson, including reading silently and aloud, listening to music, looking up Bible verses, passing things around, watching clips, looking at pictures, and experiencing physical activities.

As a leader, look ahead at your discussion questions, so you know exactly what to ask next at the first sign of a lag in the conversation. Don't be afraid to throw in a question not in the lesson plan or to tailor a question about the discussion. Tune in to students' behaviors. Watch body language closely for signs of drifting and distraction. Downturned faces, doodling, fidgeting, and blank stares all demonstrate losing interest.

Limit focus on yourself and allow students to wrestle vocally with ideas, questions, and concepts. When you allow personal time to work through topics, students often dive in deeply. I try to guide conversations minimally when kids show great interest in a topic. When students feel safe, respected, and valued, they participate.

What happens when students don't open up despite your best efforts? I found these methods work best. Try them and see.

Ask open-ended questions

Generally, avoid questions students can answer with yes, no, or one word. Instead, use open-ended questions to prompt responses. Many students are still learning communication basics, so most of the time it's easiest for them to talk about themselves.

Some of the easiest open-ended questions you can ask are "Who are you? What can you tell me about yourself?" and "What's your favorite memory from last year? Why?"

We live in a world where individuals anxiously desire acknowledgment and interest from others but rarely receive it. Don't believe me? Think of the different ways people dress, with wild hair colors and tattoos. They're dying for someone to notice them. If you recognize this deep desire for acceptance and engage it by asking personal questions, students will adore you.

Carefully avoid drawing attention to things that may embarrass students in front of others. Asking about something as simple as a bandage on their bodies in front of a group can cause an immediate shutdown from sensitive students. Even students who may laugh off a personal embarrassment may carry internal hurt and struggle to trust you.

Show real interest

Kids sniff out inauthenticity like a hound dog looking for crumbs.

In other words, they pick up on phony behavior quickly. Be genuine in how you speak to students. Show sincere care and concern. They can tell when you fake interest in what they say or when you only halfway pay attention. And it bothers them.

Show that you value their opinion, just as you would show respect to a professional when chatting. Avoid the temptation to multitask. Show courtesy by maintaining direct eye contact. Do not check your phone or watch. Do not look at other people or give in to other distractions. Nod and give verbal affirmations as you listen. Ask questions to clarify or expand your students' thinking and responses.

A little interest goes a long, long way.

Care about others more than yourself

When I was a teen, the adults in my life often frustrated me. They talked often about their world and never about mine. I listened to their stories again and again, yet they never seemed to care about my experiences. I perceived them as selfish and shallow.

Guess what? It turns out I'm not alone in finding this annoying. Teens complain about this when they confide in me. Adults may tell stories to try to connect with teens, but these efforts fail unless they engage teens to share their realities too.

Show that you care more about your students' lives than reliving your childhood. When your stories start to dominate a conversation, teens shut down more quickly than the candy aisle the day after Halloween.

In general, wait to talk about yourself until students ask you. Consider your story a form of testimony to show your kids how much you actually care about them.

Tackle challenging topics

Adults often fall into the trap of subtly shortchanging students by veering away from heady topics. Perhaps we don't feel comfortable discussing difficult topics such as love, death, politics, expectation, conflict, and sex. And we assume less-experienced kids don't want to discuss them either.

My experiences say the exact opposite.

Today's students live in a complex world, and they know they need help navigating it. We have the privilege of helping our students steer through the plethora of challenging topics they are thinking about. Don't be afraid to strap on your boots and trudge through the mire with them.

As Allison, one of my students, explains, "I want the truth about what's real, and I want to be treated respectfully and have my leaders respect me. I want to be shown how much God really loves me in a message that I understand."

Ultimately, the Word of God is powerful enough on its own. The truth is efficacious, as it is promised in Isaiah 55:11: "So shall My word be that goes out from My mouth; it shall not return to Me empty, but it shall accomplish that which I purpose, and shall succeed in the thing for which I sent it." Hebrews 4:12 says, "For the word of God is living and active, sharper than any two-edged sword, piercing to the division of soul and of spirit, of joints and of marrow, and discerning the thoughts and intentions of the heart."

Encouraging kids to open up simply readies them to hear and receive the Gospel. When we witness God's timeless truths sink into their hearts and open their eyes with newfound wonder, we find our efforts well worth the trouble.

Section 3

The "aha moment"

*No one really explained the elusive and fleeting
"aha moment" to me when I was a new youth leader.*

Maybe you can't understand "aha moments" until you find yourself in the thick of working with kids. So, maybe veterans don't try to break it into tangible concepts for greenhorn leaders. Or maybe the concept is so ephemeral that its very nature prevents logical explanation.

Either way, I found myself confronted with this reality in ministry, and I know I can't be alone.

First, let me dispel the notion that every single lesson you teach needs to be an out-of-the-park hit. I think we often fall into the trap of judging our effectiveness as Christian leaders by the reaction of our students. This is as ludicrous as telling journalists they need to convert their entire reading audience to their own personal opinions with every story they write. It's not possible.

Our job is simply to present God's eternal truths to our students: the depth of the sacrifice Christ made for us, the reality of the Father's endless love for us, the eternal glory we look forward to in heaven. We do the best we can by using the gifts God equipped us with.

Simply put, a light bulb turning on in the mind of every kid sitting in youth group or a classroom is not guaranteed.

Sometimes we feel we accomplished something if our students don't stuff cheese puffs up their noses or smack someone else in the head with a Bible.

I know several of you are nodding in agreement, aren't you? That means you work with seventh grade boys on a regular basis.

But back to this "aha moment" thing. What is it, exactly?

I define it as that moment when the Holy Spirit cracks someone in the head. You saw the light bulb turn on in her head as a significant realization dawned on her. The Word of God sank into her. She discovered a whole new section she never read before or gained new understanding of a Scripture already stored in her heart.

She experienced a moment like Cleopas and his friend spoke about when they encountered the risen Jesus on the road to Emmaus: "They said to each other, 'Did not our hearts burn within us while He talked to us on the road, while He opened to us the Scriptures?'" (Luke 24:32).

Well, maybe the Holy Spirit doesn't "crack someone in the head," but you know what I mean.

It doesn't happen every day or with every student. Sometimes it doesn't happen during a class or youth event but in the midst of conversations or circumstances of everyday life. I suspect it often occurs and we don't even realize it.

But we treasure those moments when we see a significant truth hit someone and comprehension blossoms across his face. They're like tiny slivers of heaven God allows us to see on earth. They provide small affirmations that God works through us, that the Holy Spirit flows through us to others in a very real way.

Some of the most meaningful "aha moments" occurred at times I never expected to see them.

Ironically, a life-changing "aha" occurred in a chaotic van during a mission trip. A student asked an absurd question. I jumped on it because I recognized it as a thinly disguised serious question about God. I'll never forget hearing the student utter, "Oh, wow, that's a good way to think about that." I glanced in the rearview mirror and saw comprehension dawn on his face.

"Aha moments" sometimes take months or even years to occur. I guess that's why I label them as "elusive" in my mind. They seem like rare nuggets in the endless day-to-day of our lives.

I led a small group of middle school girls for a few years. They hung out with my co-leader and me constantly, sitting with us at football games, watching movies at our houses, and eating meals with us. I witnessed their "aha moments" only after knowing some girls for three years. But realizing their rarity made those moments all the more poignant.

The other thing to realize about "aha moments"? They don't last long. At all. Especially with teenagers.

Don't be alarmed if an "aha moment" makes a student speechless, and then ten seconds later she chucks a liter of soda across the table at her friends and giggles as if nothing happened.

Something did happen. And it was important.

We're often tempted to undervalue these moments. We tell ourselves aha opportunities are too challenging, too drawn-out, or too laborious. But these brief seconds of understanding punctuate the hearts and souls of the kids we love. They change their lives, leaving indelible fingerprints on them as they grow up.

St. Peter said, "Grow in the grace and knowledge of our Lord and Savior Jesus Christ. To Him be the glory both now and to the day of eternity. Amen" (2 Peter 3:18).

In these "aha moments," our students grow in the grace and knowledge of our Lord and Savior. And they are indeed glorious.

My biggest oopsies

The smell of burnt chocolate chips and smoke wafting through the already blazing-hot room snapped a hard truth into focus. This was a mistake.

I felt sweat dripping down my forehead. I feverishly stirred chocolate and inwardly groaned as it splattered on my yellow shirt. The students around me stood in small clusters, impishly slapping their sticky peanut-butter- and chocolate-smeared hands together and shrieking with laughter as the mess dripped all over their shoes and the floor.

Our service project, cookies for friends and teachers, sat limply in the center of the room, melting by the second.

Attempting to make no-bake chocolate-covered cookies with ten- and eleven-year-olds in a room with a malfunctioning air conditioner, without wearing an apron? It was one of my biggest "oopsies" of the year.

Every so often, I like to remind myself of some of my biggest failures or mistakes just to realize how many things I learned about working with youth. Usually, they taught great lessons. Only sometimes have they resulted in painful repercussions.

Maybe this stems from being the type of person who likes to make others feel better by relating to their hurt with an even more humiliating story of my own. Or perhaps because student ministry is hard, we need to share the good, the bad, and the ugly with one another more freely. Sometimes I think we just need a good old laugh at our misfortunes to make us feel better.

Take, for instance, the time I thought it was perfectly acceptable to have two middle school boys concoct smoothies for each other using a variety of ingredients available in our youth building.

I watched the two teens mix caramel sauce, ketchup, cayenne pepper, tuna fish, hot pepper sauce, whipped cream, and more into a creamy froth. I had a reputation for playing it safe at youth events. I never pushed kids to do something they didn't want to do. But in one moment of wild abandon, I challenged the boys to race as they drank their smoothies. (After all, remember, I made money doing this trick as a kid.)

I watched one of the kids plug his nose and bend over a trash can as he tried desperately to gobble down the chunky mixture. The hotness of the pepper sauce caused tears to form in his eyes. He shouted, "I think I'm going to die!" In that moment, I realized it was probably a bad idea to allow something so gross to happen.

Another of my "oopsies" was forgetting to review our student check-in lists for transporting more than a hundred people to our annual confirmation retreat. I spent weeks planning every detail of transporting this massive group to our campsite, yet forgot the most important one—making sure every student actually showed up and got in their assigned cars.

Since we were already on the road when this dawned on me, I ended up forcing the poor students in my car to compare lists and rattle off names to me by flashlight. Luckily, everything was in order. Of course, I nearly had a panic attack, thinking we left kids behind.

And of course, I remember that fateful time I chucked a marshmallow at a group of kids who stopped by my apartment. Two empty bags of marshmallows later, my dogs actually gave up gobbling down the fluffy gut bombs. Instead, they concentrated on not puking puffy white goo all over our carpet.

Early in my ministry, brand new to an area, I took a group of kids to a laser tag center. The directions I printed were vague, so instead I trusted the claims of a seventh-grade student who insisted he knew where to go. Rolling through miles of cornfields, I realized we were utterly lost. Oops.

Sometimes I'm too careless with words. One summer, in the midst of our Vacation Bible School, the children's ministry director came to my office to talk about a little issue with a middle school student helping with the younger kids. Apparently, this student said things like "You need to sit down, or I'm going to chop your foot off." The younger kids actually felt paralyzed with fear by his threats.

The program director felt concerned and asked me where this boy could have heard such things. I gulped and admitted that he likely copied me, goofing around and issuing outlandish and sarcastic threats to my teens.

Despite the many "oopsies" I made, the Holy Spirit still works. For every cranky, worn-out, stressed, overwhelmed, angry, and overly sarcastic mistake I make, the Holy Spirit whispers to students' hearts, convicts and converts with the Word, and embeds Himself in their lives.

I strive to do my best, but I often fall short. It is comforting for me to know that God's Word is efficacious, that the Holy Spirit works even despite my failings, and that Jesus died for my sins and mess-ups too.

Ephesians 2:10 reminds me, "For we are His workmanship, created in Christ Jesus for good works, which God prepared beforehand, that we should walk in them."

Even in my biggest moments of mistake, I am still God's handiwork, created in Christ Jesus, doing the things that God prepared for me to do. And so are you.

Just take my advice and stay away from melted chocolate, marshmallows, and homemade smoothies.

Conclusion

Final words

I'm exhausted.

I worked with teenagers for four hours today. I answered emails, planned classes, and made posters for upcoming events. I picked up my dog from the vet's office and tiredly cleaned the kitchen after dinner. I responded to texts from kids, interacted with individuals online, and purchased supplies for yet another youth event.

I'm not some slick professional author, sipping lattes in an isolated office, far removed from the realities of working with kids. I don't manage a multi-million-dollar facility or work full time on lucrative book deals.

For the last half year, I came home after working a full day with kids and leaders and sat down in my home office to write this book. Many times, I propped myself up and consumed yet another cup of coffee to keep going.

I dealt with my fair share of setbacks and missed deadlines. I worried that I'm not qualified to write this book, or that I can't possibly balance everything I have on my plate without dropping something.

In other words, I'm right here with you in the thick of ministry with kids and youth.

I get you. I understand where you've been and what you've felt. I worry about the same things you feel anxious about, and I burden myself with the same frustrations. I vent about the same stuff. I feel those little breakthroughs and silent heartaches, just like you.

Sometimes the best qualified person to speak is someone just like us, smack-dab in the middle of the daily grind. We are a unique brotherhood, those who forsake the perks of high-status volunteer positions to give back to our youngest members of the community. As we give up our limited hours of free time, we directly shape the future of our world.

To be blunt, I wouldn't have wasted my time writing this book if I didn't believe our ministry to kids and youth is one of the most important things we can do with our lives.

As a teenager, I had no intention of going into ministry. I was captain of sports teams, president and founder of several clubs, ran the school newspapers, and enjoyed popularity and a thriving social life. I had everything going for me: a supportive family, tons of friends, a bright future, perfect grades, ambition, and piles of recommendations from coaches and teachers. Great universities accepted me early and offered academic scholarships. I had my future as a successful businesswoman mapped out.

By all appearances, my life was perfect.

Deep down, though, something wasn't right. I lay awake in bed for hours, staring at the ceiling with my soul rumbling uncomfortably. I couldn't shake the feeling that my plans didn't exactly line up with God's intentions for me.

One day, while driving home from cross-country practice, I pondered going into youth ministry. It seemed laughable that God would want me to serve people, someone who never attended a youth group. But over and over, through God's Word and the godly guidance of His people, I began to understand how I could serve my Lord.

I tossed the stack of acceptance letters into my drawer and concentrated on finding a program to suit my vocation. When I eventually told my friends I was going into church work, they stared at me slack-jawed, waiting for the punch line. Teachers felt confused. My family didn't understand.

No doubt you experienced something similar. People don't understand why you give your time to help others. Friends can't believe any kid could benefit from hanging out with you. Co-workers express confusion over why you give up weeknights and weekends to prepare lessons and activities for a bunch of squirmy children. Family members tell you to stop wasting your time.

Being in the trenches, working with kids and teenagers, is hard. It can be exhausting, frustrating, and irritating. Sometimes you doubt yourself. You wonder if it's really worth it and worry that your words fall on deaf ears. You may feel tempted to believe the advice of those who tell you not to waste your time or to put your efforts elsewhere. Whispers of leisure, profit, or status may swirl around you and distract you.

But in ministry, you witness firsthand the shaping of a soul for eternity.

More than any politician, diplomat, or government official, you play a vital mission in affecting the world. Through each and every life you touch, a new world of possibility and promise opens.

Within the minds of the kids we serve, a cure for cancer may exist. Someone might end racism and abuse, create a brilliant invention, write a groundbreaking book or poem, or develop a life-saving surgical procedure. Your mere words and presence may profoundly impact children and spur them toward a lifetime of service in the church, in the community, and to their country.

"My youth leader changed my life just by hanging out with me," Evan, now in college, wrote to me when he heard I was writing a book with the hope that it would help others. "It was during those times that we would have conversations about the important stuff. When my leader took time to really show that she cared about the youth by spending time with us, it made me want to follow her example. I guess this was really a principle of discipleship, intentionally spending time and modeling the way of Christ through example."

His text continued, bringing tears to my eyes. "Because of this youth leader, I came to the conclusion that I, too, wanted to lead people to follow Christ. If it hadn't been for that youth leader who changed my perspective on living the Christian life, I wouldn't be in training to be a missionary right now. After a few more years, I will be going out to another land, hoping to lead people to follow Christ, similar to how my youth leader led so many in the same way."

You are on the front lines. You impact children who will influence the entire world.

As you reach children with the grace and knowledge of what Jesus Christ did for us on the cross, faith's transformation knows no limit. Students understand, receive, believe, and follow Jesus.

Each student you encounter is different, and your loving instruction affects them in ways you can never predict. The impact may last for just one day, when they desperately need to hear something positive. Or they may be profoundly moved to make sweeping changes in their lives.

You may intercede for them in a moment when they lost all hope, save them from a tragic mistake, restore their faith in themselves, or inspire them to serve and bring others to Christ.

Through your sacrifice of time and energy, you may move a young heart in a completely new direction. You may help a student overcome an addiction, a secret heartache, an all-consuming worry, or a broken home. You may share a truth that burrows into one's soul, becoming their life purpose.

You may save a life, in this world and in eternity.

And you may not even know it, as you serve faithfully day in and day out.

Your role? To give to our youngest members of the community. Your purpose? To offer who you are, who God crafted you to be, and wherever you may be, in service to our children.

You cannot see what the future holds, but through Christ, you shape it right now.

✝